D0756919

Who Has the

Queen?

The Bridge Player's Handbook of Card Reading

FRANK STEWART

Contents

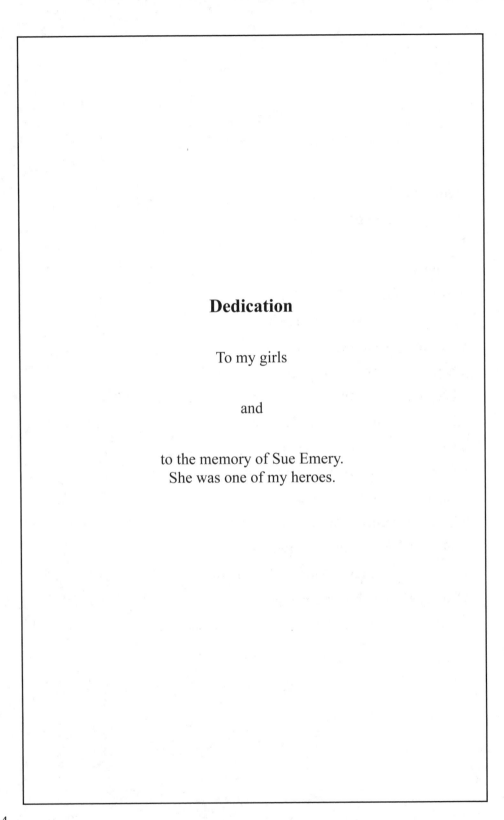

Dedication

To my girls

and

to the memory of Sue Emery.
She was one of my heroes.

Acknowledgments

Many deals in this book are adapted from "Daily Bridge Club," my syndicated column. A few have been adapted from books by other writers, whose contributions to the game and its literature I acknowledge with gratitude. Among them are H.W. Kelsey and Marshall Miles.

Richard and Mary Oshlag provided production assistance and checked the manuscript for error. Any errors that remain are my fault.

Mike Lawrence, whose books have been an inspiration to me and to many others, honored me by providing the Foreword to this book.

Foreword

Who has the queen? I have been looking for that queen for about 50 years. I have written about it in many places, and I can vouch that she is still an elusive lady.

Frank Stewart's new book "Who Has the Queen?" is full of interesting deals in which finding a missing queen, or one of her relatives, is the key to making a contract. I have been reading my copy of it and can say that it is a fun read and a learning experience at the same time -- a winning combination.

One of the things I like about this book is that it addresses the deals you see at the table almost every day you play. Goodness knows, a lot of esoteric deals make appearances in newspaper columns, but those deals do not seem to live where we play bridge. Frank's book brings you old friends and a new way to look at them.

Here is one deal that caught my eye immediately:

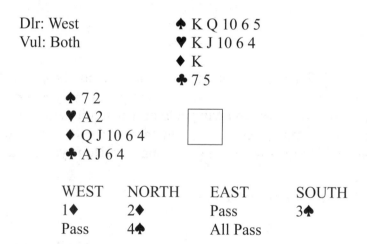

Dlr: West	♠ K Q 10 6 5
Vul: Both	♥ K J 10 6 4
	♦ K
	♣ 7 5

♠ 7 2
♥ A 2
♦ Q J 10 6 4
♣ A J 6 4

WEST	NORTH	EAST	SOUTH
1♦	2♦	Pass	3♠
Pass	4♠	All Pass	

North's 2♦ bid is the Michaels convention. A cuebid of opener's minor suit shows 5-5 in the majors and at least nine high-card points. South's 3♠ bid is invitational. North felt he had enough to bid game and he did, based on his good-quality major-suit holdings.

Dummy's ♦K wins the first trick, East playing the deuce. Dummy leads the ♥4 to declarer's queen, and West takes the ace. The key to the deal is what you do next. Do you lead clubs, hoping to take two winners there, or do you do something else?

An inference will help you here and many times in the future. If declarer had two club losers, might he not come to the ♠A to discard a club from dummy on his known ♦A? If you think South would play that way, then you should ask yourself, why did he not do that?

The answer, likely, is that he does not have the ♠A. This fact gives you the news that your partner is likely to have the ♠A. Lead a spade to partner, and he will return a club. This defense lets you set them one trick. Well done.

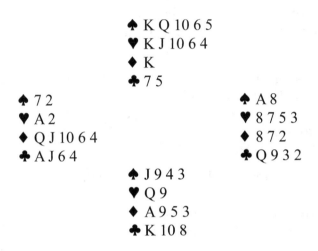

                    ♠ K Q 10 6 5
                    ♥ K J 10 6 4
                    ♦ K
                    ♣ 7 5
    ♠ 7 2   ♠ A 8
    ♥ A 2   ♥ 8 7 5 3
    ♦ Q J 10 6 4   ♦ 8 7 2
    ♣ A J 6 4   ♣ Q 9 3 2
                    ♠ J 9 4 3
                    ♥ Q 9
                    ♦ A 9 5 3
                    ♣ K 10 8

Both North and South were aggressive on this deal, but the contract was reasonable. If the defenders fail to draw the right inferences, 4♠ would succeed. If you set 4♠, you will get to hear South fuss that North bid too much. This is much nicer than letting them make 4♠ and having to listen to South tell North how nice their bidding was. Hope you liked what you heard.

I think I will read this book again.

-- Mike Lawrence

Introduction

When you learned bridge -- whether you took a class, read a book, or viewed a tutorial on the internet -- you may have been dismayed by all you had to absorb. You were obliged to learn the elements of a bidding structure -- and then, perhaps, specialized bidding methods. There were endless "rules" for the play: "second hand low" on defense, "eight ever, nine never" as declarer.

Well, if rules were all bridge had to offer, it would have no following -- much less be regarded as the greatest four-handed card game. Why do we play, anyway? Certainly not for the pleasure of memorizing a bidding system or obeying an array of rules. The game's appeal lies in problem-solving.

During a session, a player faces hundreds of decisions. Some he can resolve with little or no thought, but many require reasoning. That is what a player finds exhilarating: He has a problem and figures out the answer.

I suppose that constructing the next great bidding system amounts to problem-solving. Many players are fascinated with that aspect of the game. (In fact, a preoccupation with systems and conventions now exists that in my opinion causes many players to neglect other areas.) But for most of us, "problem-solving" suggests logical thought in the play: counting, and drawing inferences from the bidding, opening lead and later play.

That is what this book is about. It treats some of the thinking players can use when they face a "guess." Most of the ideas are simple in principle; some amount to no more than counting to 13. Players miss them because they aren't aware that the techniques exist, or because of laziness or a lack of focus.

The 12 chapters cover various types of logical thinking, presented as problems. Assume IMP scoring unless matchpoints is specified. See how many problems you can solve. My hope is that through this book, you will come to realize how much fun bridge can be to play well.

Frank Stewart

Fayette, AL

July 2011

Author's note

The bidding in this book is natural -- basically "Standard" -- but it follows no explicit style, nor do I advocate all of the actions stipulated. Differences in bidding judgment are part of the game; and after all, the focus is on the play.

Opening bids of 1NT show 16 to 18 HCP, though in a few problems a player may open 1NT with 15. Some conventional methods do make an appearance. A modern tendency is to play jump-raises of overcalls as preemptive, but occasionally I have a player offering such a raise as constructive. In other auctions, a player may not use a "transfer" response to 1NT or 2NT when that would be the choice of many players.

A few of the problems revisit a theme introduced earlier. I won't apologize for that: Repetition is an effective learning tool.

CHAPTER 1

Who has the queen?

Pietro Forquet of Italy, a many-time world champion and a superb declarer, used to complain that finding missing queens was his great weakness. Perhaps you always misguess also; it's the story of your life.

A two-way guess for a missing queen is a 50-50 proposition in theory, but a capable declarer should guess right, by my estimate, 80 percent of the time. Experts occasionally rely on an instinctive "feel of the table," but usually clues from the bidding and play will point the way.

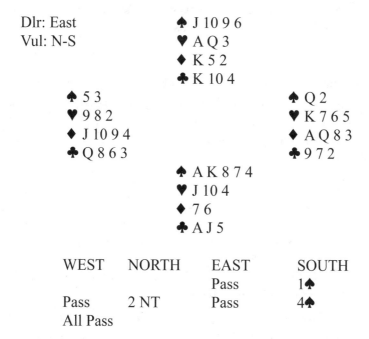

```
Dlr: East          ♠ J 10 9 6
Vul: N-S           ♥ A Q 3
                   ♦ K 5 2
                   ♣ K 10 4

    ♠ 5 3                        ♠ Q 2
    ♥ 9 8 2                      ♥ K 7 6 5
    ♦ J 10 9 4                   ♦ A Q 8 3
    ♣ Q 8 6 3                    ♣ 9 7 2

                   ♠ A K 8 7 4
                   ♥ J 10 4
                   ♦ 7 6
                   ♣ A J 5
```

WEST	NORTH	EAST	SOUTH
		Pass	1♠
Pass	2 NT	Pass	4♠
All Pass			

North's 2NT response is a conventional forcing spade raise.

West leads the ♦J, winning. East wins the next diamond with the queen and tries to cash the ace. South ruffs and takes the ♠AK, dropping the queen. A heart finesse loses to East, who returns a heart to dummy. Now if South can bring himself to count to 13, he will know who has the ♣Q: East, who passed as dealer, has shown the ♦AQ, ♥K and ♠Q.

Those are the kinds of simple inferences that experienced players rely on. This chapter introduces several related techniques. Nothing about them is abstruse, but players miss them, usually due to a lack of focus.

```
Dlr: West          ♠ J 9 6 5 3
Vul: N-S           ♥ K J 5
                   ♦ A Q
                   ♣ J 4 3


                   ♠ K Q 10 7 4
                   ♥ A 10 4
                   ♦ 7 6
                   ♣ Q 6 5
```

WEST	NORTH	EAST	SOUTH
1♣	Pass	Pass	1♠
Pass	3♠	Pass	4♠
All Pass			

West cashes the ♣KA and leads a third club; luckily for you, your queen wins. You lead the ♠K, and West takes the ace. East discards a diamond. West shifts to a diamond, and dummy's queen wins. You draw trumps -- East discards two more diamonds -- and cash the ♦A. Both defenders play low.

Who has the ♥Q?

****

West started with three spades and three or four clubs: six or seven black cards, hence six or seven red cards. His red cards should be divided 4-3, 4-2 or 3-3; he had four clubs at most, and with a five-card suit, he would have opened in it. So West's pattern was balanced.

Moreover, you've seen West show 14 HCP: ♣AK, ♠A, ♦K. Make an assumption: If West had the ♥Q in his balanced hand, what would his opening bid have been?

Play East for the ♥Q.

```
♠ A 8 2                    ♠
♥ 7 6 3                    ♥ Q 9 8 2
♦ K 8 2                    ♦ J 10 9 5 4 3
♣ A K 10 8                 ♣ 9 7 2
```

```
Dlr: East          ♠ 9 3
Vul: N-S           ♥ A J 9 6
                   ♦ A 7 6 4
                   ♣ K 5 4


                   ♠ K 6
                   ♥ K Q 10 8 4 2
                   ♦ 8
                   ♣ A J 10 2
```

WEST	NORTH	EAST	SOUTH
		1♠	2♥
2♠	3♠	Pass	4♣
Pass	4♦	Pass	6♥
All Pass			

West leads the ♠2, and East takes the ace and returns the queen to your king. Suppose you (correctly) take the ♦A, ruff a diamond and lead a trump to dummy, on which West discards a spade. You ruff another diamond, lead a trump to dummy (club from West) and ruff the last diamond, as both defenders follow. You draw East's last trump, and West discards another spade.

Your last four cards are the ♣AJ102, and dummy has a trump and ♣K54. Who has the ♣Q?

****

You have a complete count of the distribution. West started with four spades, no hearts and four diamonds; hence five clubs. East was 5-3-4-1. Take the ♣A to see which club East has. If it's not the queen, finesse through West.

```
♠ 10 8 4 2              ♠ A Q J 7 5
♥                       ♥ 7 5 3
♦ J 9 5 2               ♦ K Q 10 3
♣ Q 9 8 7 6             ♣ 3
```

Some players would have bid more than 2♠ with the West cards.

```
Dlr: East          ♠ J 9 7 4
Vul: N-S           ♥ K 4
                   ♦ Q 8 6
                   ♣ K 10 6 5


                   ♠ K Q 10 6 5
                   ♥ 8 3
                   ♦ A
                   ♣ A J 9 4 2
```

WEST	NORTH	EAST	SOUTH
		1♥	1♠
Pass	2♠	Pass	4♠
All Pass			

Your jump to 4♠ was mildly aggressive, but your side is vulnerable (with more to gain by scoring game), and your two-suiter becomes powerful once North supports the spades. If he has no more than the ♠A and ♣Q, you are a favorite for 10 tricks.

West leads the ♥2, and East takes the ace and queen. He shifts to the ♠A and another spade, and West follows. Trumps are drawn.

To get it over with, you lead to the ♣K and return a club. East plays the eight. Do you finesse or put up the ace?

****

East doesn't need the ♣Q for his opening bid; he might hold the ♦K in addition to the ♥AQ and ♠A. Instead, put yourself in West's place and consider the defense. If you finesse, you are playing East for ♣Q83, West for a singleton. But suppose West had a singleton club and knew that East, who opened the bidding, had values that probably included an ace or two. What would West's opening lead have been?

Put up the ♣A.

```
♠ 8 3                    ♠ A 2
♥ 10 7 5 2               ♥ A Q J 9 6
♦ J 9 4 3 2              ♦ K 10 7 5
♣ Q 7                    ♣ 8 3
```

If West had a singleton club, an easy defense would have beaten your contract.

```
Dlr: South          ♠ A 7 2
Vul: None           ♥ J 8
                    ♦ J 9 5 3 2
                    ♣ 9 6 3


                    ♠ K Q J
                    ♥ Q 6 4
                    ♦ A K 10 6
                    ♣ K J 4
```

WEST	NORTH	EAST	SOUTH
			1♦
2♣	2♦	Pass	3 NT
All Pass			

West leads the ♥2, and East takes the ace and shifts to the ♣10: jack, queen. West cashes the ♣A and leads a third club to your king, as East pitches the ♥3.

You cash the ♦A; both defenders play low. What next?

****

West had five clubs and four hearts. (If East had five hearts, he would have returned a heart.) To get a count on the diamonds, cash your spade tricks, ending with dummy's ace.

Suppose East-West follow. Now you know that West's pattern was 3-4-1-5, so a finesse with your ten on the second diamond is marked.

```
        ♠ 9 6 4              ♠ 10 8 5 3
        ♥ K 10 5 2           ♥ A 9 7 3
        ♦ 4                  ♦ Q 8 7
        ♣ A Q 8 7 5          ♣ 10 2
```

If West turned up with only two spades, you would play to drop the ♦Q.

Dlr: West
Vul: None

♠ A 4 3
♥ 9 6 4
♦ Q 10 6 5
♣ K 10 4

♠ K 7
♥ A 8 2
♦ 7 4 3
♣ A J 9 6 5

WEST	NORTH	EAST	SOUTH
1♦	Pass	1♥	2♣
2♥	3♣	All Pass	

You were absent when they passed out fear, so you overcall 2♣ as South. To act between two bidding opponents is risky, and the prospect of gaining anything is uncertain; but this time you survive when North supports your clubs, and you buy the contract at 3♣.

West leads the ♦KA, and East discards a spade. East ruffs the next diamond, as dummy plays the ten, and shifts to a low heart. You take the ace and can make the contract if you pick up the trumps. (The ♦Q will furnish a heart discard.)

Who has the ♣Q?

****

An inferential count is available. West started with five diamonds, East with one. Hearts ... were 3-4: East needed four to bid the suit, West needed three-card support to raise. Spades ... must have been 4-4. West would have opened 1♠ with five, East would have responded 1♠ with five.

So East's pattern was 4-4-1-4. Lead a club to the king. If West follows low, let the ♣10 ride.

♠ J 9 8 2
♥ K J 3
♦ A K J 8 2
♣ 2

♠ Q 10 6 5
♥ Q 10 7 5
♦ 9
♣ Q 8 7 3

```
Dlr: West          ♠ 9 6 3
Vul: N-S           ♥ A 6 2
                   ♦ K Q 5 2
                   ♣ A 7 5


                   ♠ J 5
                   ♥ K J 8 7 4
                   ♦ 8 7 4
                   ♣ K Q 3
```

WEST	NORTH	EAST	SOUTH
1♠	Pass	Pass	2♥
Pass	4♥	All Pass	

When the opponents stop at the one level, you balance with 2♥ on a light hand. North's raise to game is bold; you were counting on him for significant values when you balanced.

West leads the ♣4: five, jack, king. You lead a trump to the ace, both defenders playing low, and return a trump. East follows with the nine.

Who has the queen?

****

West's opening lead was unexpected. Surely he would have led a high spade with a suit headed by the A-K, K-Q-10 or even K-Q. Since East is marked with a high spade plus the ♣J, he can't have the ♥Q. Then he would have held enough points to respond to the opening bid.

Put up the ♥K and hope the queen falls. Then you will draw East's last trump and lead twice toward dummy's diamond honors, hoping to lose only two spades and one diamond.

```
♠ A Q 10 7 2          ♠ K 8 4
♥ Q 3                 ♥ 10 9 5
♦ A J 10              ♦ 9 6 3
♣ 10 8 4              ♣ J 9 6 2
```

```
Dlr: West          ♠ K J 9 6
Vul: Both          ♥ K 6 2
                   ♦ Q 10 5 4
                   ♣ 9 4


                   ♠ A 10 7 5 2
                   ♥ 8 5
                   ♦ A K 9 7
                   ♣ 10 5
```

WEST	NORTH	EAST	SOUTH
Pass	Pass	Pass	1♠
Pass	3♠	Pass	4♠
All Pass			

Questionable contracts are often reached when both players take an aggressive view, lusting after a vulnerable game bonus. North's raise to 3♠ was borderline at best. Your 4♠ was optimistic; perhaps you hoped to ruff diamonds in dummy.

West leads the ♣K and next the ♣7 to East's ace. East shifts to the ♦8, which rides to dummy's ten.

Who has the ♠Q?

****

To have a chance, you must assume that West has the ♥A. But he has already shown the ♣KQ and ♦J (and someone has the ♣J and ♥J). So you must give East the ♠Q. Cash the king and finesse through East.

```
♠ 4                    ♠ Q 8 3
♥ A 10 4               ♥ Q J 9 7 3
♦ J 6 3 2              ♦ 8
♣ K Q 8 7 3            ♣ A J 6 2
```

At matchpoints, you might play the same way. If you knew every North-South would reach 4♠, your object would be not to make the contract but to take more tricks than the other Souths. Hence you might reasonably judge to play for the drop in trumps. But as it is, many -- perhaps most -- pairs will stop at a partscore, so you might play to make your game.

```
Dlr: South          ♠ K J 2
Vul: Both           ♥ K 6 5
                    ♦ K 10 8 3 2
                    ♣ 8 3


                    ♠ Q 4 3
                    ♥ A J 7 2
                    ♦ A J 7 4
                    ♣ A 5
```

WEST	NORTH	EAST	SOUTH
			1 NT
Pass	3 NT	All Pass	

West hits you where it hurts by leading the ♣2. East plays the king, and you take your ace immediately.

If you could sneak by with a spade trick, five diamond tricks would give you nine. But suppose you adopt the technically defensible play of leading to the ♥K and back to your jack. West plays low but discards a spade on the ♥A.

How do you play the diamonds?

****

West had four clubs, from his lead of the deuce, and two hearts. If he held five spades, even lacking the ace, his opening lead would have been a spade. Therefore, play West for no more than four spades and at least three diamonds. Take the ♦A, intending to finesse with the ten next.

```
♠ 9 7 6 5              ♠ A 10 8
♥ 8 4                  ♥ Q 10 9 3
♦ Q 9 5                ♦ 6
♣ Q 10 6 2             ♣ K J 9 7 4
```

Dlr: West   ♠ K 10 9 5
Vul: Both   ♥ Q 7 6 5
                ♦ 5 3 2
                ♣ J 10

                ♠ A J 8 3
                ♥ 10 4
                ♦ Q J 7
                ♣ K Q 5 2

WEST	NORTH	EAST	SOUTH
Pass	Pass	Pass	1♣
Pass	1♥	Pass	1♠
Pass	2♠	All Pass	

North might have passed South at 1♠. Although opener's non-jump rebid in a new suit is not forcing, a few pairs treat a 1♠ rebid as forcing.

West leads the ♥K and shifts to a diamond. East takes the king and ace and leads a third diamond, and your queen wins.

To make 2♠, you must draw trumps without loss. Who has the ♠Q? If you don't know, can you find out?

****

West has the ♥AK, East has the ♦AK, and neither player opened the bidding. So he who hath the ♣A hath not the ♠Q. To solve your trump problem, lead a club to smoke out the ace.

     ♠ 6 4 2   ♠ Q 7
     ♥ A K 9 3   ♥ J 8 2
     ♦ 10 8 6   ♦ A K 9 4
     ♣ A 7 6   ♣ 9 8 4 3

Dlr: South	♠ Q
Vul: Both	♥ Q 6
Matchpoints	♦ K J 9 8 6 5 4
	♣ K 7 2

```
                    ♠ A K 3
                    ♥ 10 8 5 4
                    ♦ A 2
                    ♣ A Q 6 5
```

WEST	NORTH	EAST	SOUTH
			1 NT
Pass	3 NT	All Pass	

North's raise to 3NT is understandable at matchpoints. A diamond contract might be safer, but notrump is the higher-scoring strain. North-South will get a zero if they are +600 or +620 at 5♦ when other pairs are +630 or +660 at notrump. (North-South could make 6♦ when South has an ideal hand such as xxx,Axx,Axx,AQJx, but partners seldom hold exactly the right cards.)

West leads the ♥2. East takes the king and ace and leads a third heart, and West scores his nine and jack. Dummy discards diamonds. West then exits with a spade to dummy's queen.

You try three high clubs: If the suit breaks 3-3, you have nine tricks. West discards a spade. Then all follow to the ♠AK.

How do you attack the diamonds?

****

West had four hearts and two clubs. If he had a five-card spade suit, his opening lead would have been a spade. Play West for 4-4-3-2 pattern: Take the ♦A, planning to finesse with the jack.

♠ 10 8 5 2	♠ J 9 7 6 4
♥ J 9 3 2	♥ A K 7
♦ Q 10 7	♦ 3
♣ 9 3	♣ J 10 8 4

```
Dlr: West          ♠ A 5 3
Vul: N-S           ♥ K 9 6 2
                   ♦ J 6 4 3
                   ♣ Q 6


                   ♠ 10 8 2
                   ♥ A J 10 5 3
                   ♦ A K 10
                   ♣ 10 2
```

WEST	NORTH	EAST	SOUTH
1♠	Pass	Pass	2♥
Pass	3♥	Pass	4♥
All Pass			

North's raise to 3♥ was a big stretch. This time you hold a sound balancing overcall and can go on to game, but the contract is poor. You need to manage both red suits.

West leads the ♠6. Who has the ♥Q? Who has the ♦Q?

****

East must have a spade honor since West would have led the king from K-Q-J-x-x or K-Q-x-x-x. East must also have a club honor since West would have led a high club if he held the A-K. So West holds both red queens, otherwise East would have had enough to respond to 1♠.

```
♠ K J 7 6 4          ♠ Q 9
♥ Q 8 4              ♥ 7
♦ Q 7                ♦ 9 8 5 2
♣ A J 5              ♣ K 9 8 7 4 3
```

After you take the ♥A, you will let the ♥J ride through West and play to drop the singleton or doubleton ♦Q.

I suspect many players would have scraped up a response with the actual East hand.

Dlr: South
Vul: N-S

♠ Q 5
♥ K 9 5 3
♦ 8 4
♣ K Q J 8 4

♠ A K J 7 3
♥ A J 10 8
♦ A Q
♣ 5 3

WEST	NORTH	EAST	SOUTH
			1♠
Pass	2♣	Pass	2♥
Pass	4♥	Pass	6♥
All Pass			

West leads the ♣A and shifts to a diamond. You capture East's king. Who has the ♥Q?

****

You seem to have an outright guess, but for West to cash the ace of dummy's bid suit is suspicious. After the auction you had, a diamond lead would be normal, hoping to set up a diamond trick before you forced out the ♣A and used the clubs for discards.

Perhaps West thought he had a possible trump trick and would beat the slam if his ♣A cashed. Play him for the ♥Q.

♠ 10 9 8   ♠ 6 4 2
♥ Q 7 6   ♥ 4 2
♦ J 9 5 2   ♦ K 10 7 6 3
♣ A 9 2   ♣ 10 7 6

```
Dlr: West          ♠ A 9 2
Vul: None          ♥ A J 3
                   ♦ 8 5
                   ♣ 9 6 4 3 2


                   ♠ J 6
                   ♥ K 9 8 6 4 2
                   ♦ 10 3
                   ♣ A K J
```

WEST	NORTH	EAST	SOUTH
Pass	Pass	Pass	1♥
Pass	2♥	Dbl	3♥
Pass	4♥	All Pass	

You thought your re-raise to 3♥ was obstructive. (Many pairs do treat it that way; with a strong hand and game interest, South could redouble or bid a new suit.) But North thought you were trying for game and lands you at a shaky 4♥ contract.

West leads the ♦2. East takes the king and ace and shifts to the ♠4: six, ten, ace.

Who has the ♥Q? Who has the ♣Q?

****

East's double suggests heart shortness, but other indications are available. East has the ♦AKJ; West would have led the queen from Q-J-x-x. East also has a spade honor since West would have led a spade from K-Q-10-x. Few Easts would pass in third position, not vulnerable, with a hand such as Q874,7,AKJ76,Q85.

Lead a trump to your king, intending to finesse with dummy's jack on the way back. Later, you will cash the ♣AK, hoping to drop West's queen.

```
         ♠ K 10 5 3              ♠ Q 8 7 4
         ♥ Q 10 5               ♥ 7
         ♦ Q 9 4 2             ♦ A K J 7 6
         ♣ Q 7                  ♣ 10 8 5
```

Dlr: North   ♠ A K J 7 4 3 2
Vul: Both   ♥ Q 7 4
                  ♦ 7 4
                  ♣ 9

                  ♠ 8 5
                  ♥ A K J 10
                  ♦ A K J 10
                  ♣ A K 6

WEST	NORTH	EAST	SOUTH
	1♠	Pass	3♥
Pass	3♠	Pass	4♦
Pass	4♥	Pass	5♣
Pass	6♥	Pass	7♥
All Pass			

The auction is vintage; indeed, this deal arose more than 70 years ago. Modern players might respond 2♦ as South, saving room to look for a trump suit and investigate for a grand slam. Nevertheless, the actual auction was effective. The 7♥ contract is sound.

West leads the ♣4 to East's queen and your ace. You ruff a club in dummy and cash the ♠A, then take the ♦AK and lead the ♦J. West discards a club, so you ruff in dummy and take four rounds of trumps. East follows, West discards two more clubs.

When you cash the ♣K, both defenders follow. At trick 12, you lead a spade, and West plays the nine. Do you play the king or the jack from dummy?

****

It's no problem. West had two hearts and two diamonds. Both he and East followed suit to three club leads, and West discarded three more clubs on your red-suit leads. You have accounted for 10 of West's cards, so he had three spades. Finesse with the ♠J.

♠ Q 9 6   ♠ 10
♥ 9 6   ♥ 8 5 3 2
♦ 9 5   ♦ Q 8 6 3 2
♣ J 8 5 4 3 2   ♣ Q 10 7

Dlr: North   ♠ A 6 3
Vul: None   ♥ K 10 5
                ♦ Q 2
                ♣ A 9 7 6 3

                ♠ J 8 7 4 2
                ♥ A J 9 8 3 2
                ♦
                ♣ 5 4

WEST	NORTH	EAST	SOUTH
	1♣	Pass	1♥
Pass	2♥	Pass	4♥
All Pass			

Once you found the heart fit, you could afford to jump to game. You could expect to take 11 tricks opposite a skimpy North hand such as 53,K1054,876,AK83, and -- who knows? -- even in this day of ever-lighter opening bids, he might have more than that.

West leads the ♦J: queen, king, ruff. You lead the ♠A and a second spade, and East takes the king and shifts to the ♣2: four, jack, ace. West wins the next spade, cashes the ♣K and leads another diamond that you ruff.

How do you play the trumps?

****

Take stock of the evidence. East had ♠K9, apparently ♣Q1082 and some number of diamonds headed by the A-K. He had enough high-card values to act over 1♣ but passed; but if East had a five-card diamond suit, he could have overcalled. Play East for 2-3-4-4 pattern. Lead a trump to the king and back to your jack.

        ♠ Q 10 5   ♠ K 9
        ♥ 4   ♥ Q 7 6
        ♦ J 10 9 6 5 4 3   ♦ A K 8 7
        ♣ K J   ♣ Q 10 8 2

The problems in this set have illustrated finding a missing queen through techniques of counting, inference, assumption and discovery. Later chapters treat each of these areas individually.

CHAPTER 2

Assumption

I've heard assumption defined as the mother of all screw-ups. But assumptions at bridge are necessary and can actually simplify card reading. To make or defeat the contract, a player must often assume that the cards lie a certain way.

When you take a finesse, you assume it will work, but most assumptions are more delicate. Some are "second-degree," as Terence Reese named them, meaning that they follow logically from an earlier assumption about the location of another missing card. For instance, if you need a missing honor to be favorably placed, assume it is. Then follow the consequences of your assumption.

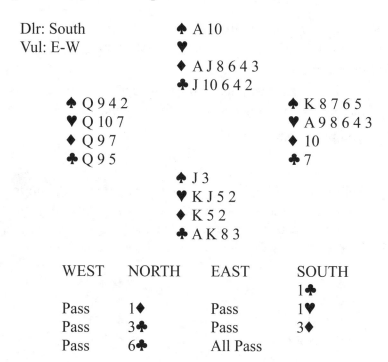

Dlr: South		♠ A 10	
Vul: E-W		♥	
		♦ A J 8 6 4 3	
		♣ J 10 6 4 2	

♠ Q 9 4 2	♠ K 8 7 6 5
♥ Q 10 7	♥ A 9 8 6 4 3
♦ Q 9 7	♦ 10
♣ Q 9 5	♣ 7

	♠ J 3
	♥ K J 5 2
	♦ K 5 2
	♣ A K 8 3

WEST	NORTH	EAST	SOUTH
			1♣
Pass	1♦	Pass	1♥
Pass	3♣	Pass	3♦
Pass	6♣	All Pass	

West finds the best lead of a spade against 6♣. South takes the ace and cashes the ♣AK, but East discards. Declarer then takes the ♦K and leads a second diamond.

When West follows with the seven and nine, declarer must finesse. His only chance is that West, with the high trump, must follow to three diamond leads so declarer can discard his losing spade on the fourth diamond. A 2-2 diamond break won't help.

Dlr: West   ♠ A J 7
Vul: Both   ♥ 9 7 6 4 2
                 ♦ K J 3
                 ♣ 10 3

                 ♠ Q 10 6 2
                 ♥ K Q 10 8 3
                 ♦ 9 4
                 ♣ A J

WEST	NORTH	EAST	SOUTH
Pass	Pass	Pass	1♥
2♣	4♥	All Pass	

North's leap to game is a compliment to your dummy play; a limit raise to 3♥ would have been plenty. But an overbidding partner has the benefit of forcing you to sharpen your play.

West leads a low club, East puts up the king, and you take the ace. When you lead the ♥K, West wins, cashes the ♣Q and leads a diamond.

What do you play from dummy?

****

It's not likely that West would lead from the ♦Q; if your diamonds were A-10-x, he would save you a guess. Nevertheless, you must play the ♦J. To make the contract, you must assume the spade finesse will work. But if West had ♠K, ♥A, ♦A and ♣Q, he would have opened the bidding.

      ♠ K 8 3   ♠ 9 5 4
      ♥ A   ♥ J 5
      ♦ Q 8 2   ♦ A 10 7 6 5
      ♣ Q 8 7 6 5 2   ♣ K 9 4

Dlr: North
Vul: N-S

♠ 8 6 4 3
♥ A 7
♦ A K 3 2
♣ K 6 5

♠ K
♥ K J 6 5 3 2
♦ Q 5 4
♣ 9 4 2

WEST	NORTH	EAST	SOUTH
	1♦	1♠	2♥
2♠	Pass	Pass	3♥
Pass	4♥	All Pass	

North's raise to 4♥ looks odd: In effect, you had a choice between playing at 4♥ or trying to beat 2♠. But North figured you had a spade singleton, and all his high-card values looked good.

West leads the ♠2, and East takes the ace and shifts to the ♣J. West wins and returns the ♣Q, and East ruffs dummy's king and leads another spade. You ruff and lead a trump to the ace, as both defenders follow low. On the next trump, East plays low again.

Do you finesse with the jack or put up your king?

****

Finesse. You need a discard for your club loser and so must hope for a 3-3 diamond break. But West started with six clubs and at least three spades, so to have a chance, you must give him a singleton trump.

♠ J 9 2	♠ A Q 10 7 5
♥ 10	♥ Q 9 8 4
♦ J 7 6	♦ 10 9 8
♣ A Q 10 8 7 3	♣ J

29

```
Dlr: North          ♠ 6 4 2
Vul: Both           ♥ 7 6
                    ♦ Q J 10 8
                    ♣ A Q 9 4


                    ♠ A K Q
                    ♥ K 5 2
                    ♦ A 5 3
                    ♣ J 10 7 6
```

WEST	NORTH	EAST	SOUTH
	Pass	Pass	1 NT
Pass	3 NT	All Pass	

Against your prosaic 3NT, West leads the ♠10. You win and let the ♣J ride, and East takes the king and shifts to the dreaded ♥Q. You play low, and next comes the ♥J.

Do you duck again or cover?

****

You must assume that the diamond finesse will work and can assume that East has no more than five hearts. (He would have opened 1♥ or 2♥ with J3,AQJ1083,762,K3, so you can rule out that possibility. If he has J3,QJ10983,762,K3, you will make 3NT no matter what you do.) But if East has the ♦K, he can't have the ♥AQJ and the ♣K; he passed in second position.

You should duck the second heart.

```
♠ 10 9 8 7              ♠ J 5 3
♥ A 9 4                 ♥ Q J 10 8 3
♦ 9 4 2                 ♦ K 7 6
♣ 8 5 2                 ♣ K 3
```

West will win the third heart, but the defense will take no more tricks.

Dlr: North   ♠ A Q 8
Vul: N-S   ♥ J 7 4
                 ♦ A J 7 2
                 ♣ A 5 3

                 ♠ K J 10 9 7
                 ♥ A 6 3
                 ♦ 6
                 ♣ K Q 10 4

WEST	NORTH	EAST	SOUTH
	1 NT	Pass	3♠
Pass	4♠	Pass	5♥
Pass	6♠	All Pass	

West leads a trump -- good for the defense. With a red-suit lead, you could have tried for a dummy reversal, but the trump lead removes a necessary entry to dummy.

Suppose you take the ♦A, ruff a diamond and lead a low heart to dummy's jack and East's queen. If East led a diamond, you could still reverse the dummy, but he returns a heart to your ace. You lead a second trump to dummy, and when both defenders follow, you ruff another diamond, as East follows with the king.

Next you cash the ♣KA and, at the 10th trick, lead a third club from dummy. East follows low; no jack has appeared. What do you play from your hand?

****

Finesse with the ten. Your only chance is to pitch a heart from dummy on your fourth club, then ruff your losing heart in dummy. You must find East with four clubs as well as the missing trump. If West started with J-9-7, the contract is unmakable.

     ♠ 5 4   ♠ 6 3 2
     ♥ K 10 5 2   ♥ Q 9 8
     ♦ Q 9 8 5 4   ♦ K 10 3
     ♣ 9 7   ♣ J 8 6 2

If this deal arose at matchpoints, I suspect North-South would do well not to bid slam. If winning 12 tricks requires skillful play (as here), not to mention luck, North-South will get a good result for either +680 or +1430.

```
Dlr: West          ♠ K 6
Vul: N-S           ♥ K 9 6 4 2
                   ♦ 7 2
                   ♣ K J 5 3


                   ♠ Q 10 4
                   ♥ A Q J 7 3
                   ♦ A Q 5
                   ♣ 6 2
```

WEST	NORTH	EAST	SOUTH
Pass	Pass	Pass	1♥
Dbl	Redbl	1♠	Pass
Pass	2♥	Pass	4♥
All Pass			

North's bid of 2♥ was conservative. The bidding improved the value of his black-suit kings since if South didn't have the aces, West probably did. North could have jumped to 3♥, especially since he was a passed hand.

West leads a trump, and you take the A-Q. West had a singleton. You lead a spade to the king and return a spade to your ten. West wins with the jack and leads a low club.

What do you play from dummy?

****

Your contract is safe if East has the ♦K, so assume the worst: that West has it. Then West, a passed hand, won't have ♣A in addition to his ♠AJ.

You should play the ♣J. If you have misguessed -- East wins with the queen and returns a club to West's ace -- you will make 4♥ anyway because the diamond finesse will work.

```
     ♠ A J 7 2            ♠ 9 8 5 3
     ♥ 10                 ♥ 8 5
     ♦ K J 9 4            ♦ 10 8 6 3
     ♣ Q 9 7 4            ♣ A 10 8
```

If after West took the ♠J, he led the ♠A, forcing dummy to ruff, you would have finessed in diamonds next, learning that West had the king. Then you would know he couldn't have the ♣A. So West's club shift was dangerous but a good play as the cards lay: He forced you to take a premature view of the club position.

```
Dlr: West          ♠ J 6 4 2
Vul: N-S           ♥ K 10 7
                   ♦ 8 6 2
                   ♣ A J 5


                   ♠ A
                   ♥ A Q J 2
                   ♦ K 9
                   ♣ Q 10 9 8 6 2
```

WEST	NORTH	EAST	SOUTH
Pass	Pass	Pass	1♣
1♠	1 NT	Pass	2♥
Pass	3♣	Pass	4♣
Pass	5♣	All Pass	

You had a difficult hand to describe. Some players would have wanted more high-card points to reverse to 2♥ -- but maybe not after North's value-showing bid of 1NT. You did well to reach a club contract since a diamond lead against 3NT by North might have been fatal.

Against 5♣, West leads the ♠K, and your ace wins. You lead the ♣Q, and West plays low. What do you do?

****

Perhaps you believe that "If they don't cover, they don't have it," but no West would cover the ♣Q after your bidding suggested long, strong clubs. Still, you should put up the ♣A. If West has the king, you will make your game anyway since East will have the ♦A. West would have opened with the ♦A, ♣K and five spades headed by the K-Q.

You must guard against the actual East-West layout:

```
♠ K Q 9 7 3          ♠ 10 8 5
♥ 9 6                ♥ 8 5 4 3
♦ A J 5              ♦ Q 10 7 4 3
♣ 7 4 3              ♣ K
```

```
Dlr: East              ♠ K 7
Vul: N-S               ♥ A K 4 2
                       ♦ J 9 6 5
                       ♣ J 10 8


                       ♠ J 4
                       ♥ 8 5 3
                       ♦ A Q 10 4
                       ♣ A Q 9 7
```

WEST	NORTH	EAST	SOUTH
		Pass	1♣
Pass	1♥	Pass	1 NT
Pass	3 NT	All Pass	

Your auction looks reasonable enough (in real life, it was conducted by a world-class pair), but it landed you at a poor 3NT -- and from the wrong side. Some Souths would have opened 1♦ and bid 2♣ over a major-suit response; I dislike that plan because it not only misrepresents the pattern but fails to limit the strength quickly.

A few Souths would raise the 1♥ response to 2♥. Then North might try 2NT next, and North-South would stop there. Given the skimpy hands that some players treat as opening bids, North might also have settled for 2NT instead of 3NT.

Anyway, West leads the ♠2. What do you play from dummy?

****

This looks grim. You must guess right in spades and win the minor-suit finesses. Well, if East has both minor-suit kings, he is unlikely to have five spades to the ace as well. He wouldn't have opened the bidding but would have had an easy 1♠ overcall at his second turn. Put up the ♠K.

```
♠ A 10 6 2          ♠ Q 9 8 5 3
♥ Q 10 9            ♥ J 7 6
♦ 8 7 2            ♦ K 3
♣ 6 4 2            ♣ K 5 3
```

In a major event 30 years ago, the late Bobby Goldman made the correct assumptions and brought home the contract.

34

Dlr: North   ♠ A J 7 6 2
Vul: N-S   ♥ 7 5 3
                  ♦ K 5
                  ♣ Q 10 2

                  ♠ K Q 10 8 5
                  ♥ K J
                  ♦ 8 6 4
                  ♣ A J 4

WEST	NORTH	EAST	SOUTH
	Pass	Pass	1♠
Pass	3♠	Pass	4♠
All Pass			

West leads the ♦J, and East takes the ace and queen and shifts to the ♥2.

Do you play the king or the jack?

****

The problem illustrates "second-degree assumption." To hold your losers to three, you need East to hold the ♣K, so assume he does. But East is a passed hand and has shown the ♦AQ, so you can't assign him the ♥A as well.

Play the ♥J. You must hope West has the ace and East has the queen.

    ♠ 4   ♠ 9 3
    ♥ A 9 8 6   ♥ Q 10 4 2
    ♦ J 10 9 3 2   ♦ A Q 7
    ♣ 9 6 5   ♣ K 8 7 3

Dlr: East
Vul: None

♠ A Q 9 7 2
♥ J 7 6 3
♦ A 7 3
♣ Q

♠ K 6 4
♥ A K 9 8 4
♦ 9 4 2
♣ A 7

WEST	NORTH	EAST	SOUTH
		3♣	3♥
Pass	4♣	Pass	4♥
Pass	6♥	All Pass	

You had a minimum -- some would say a subminimum -- for your 3♥ overcall. North's 4♣ was a try for slam. He seems to have accepted his own try, but perhaps he had enough values to bid slam.

Your 6♥ contract would be a good spot with a club opening lead, but West leads the ♦Q. You take dummy's ace, and East signals with the eight. When you cash the ♥AK, East discards a club.

How do you handle the spades?

****

A 3-2 spade break will avail nothing. Even if West has three, he will ruff the fourth spade and cash a diamond. To succeed, you must find West with four spades. Take the ♠K. If both defenders play low, lead to dummy's nine.

♠ J 10 8 5   ♠ 3
♥ Q 10 2   ♥ 5
♦ Q J 10   ♦ K 8 6 5
♣ J 9 4   ♣ K 10 8 6 5 3 2

True, you are risking two extra undertricks at 50 points apiece, but if you go down at a makable slam by missing the correct technical play, the psychological damage to you and your partnership will be significant.

At matchpoints, take your best play to make the slam. Not many pairs will reach 6♥. Down three will score no matchpoints, but down one will score almost none.

```
Dlr: East            ♠ 7 6 4 3
Vul: None            ♥ J 10 4
                     ♦ 9 8 7 2
                     ♣ A K


                     ♠ A Q J 2
                     ♥ Q 6 2
                     ♦ K Q 6
                     ♣ Q J 4
```

WEST	NORTH	EAST	SOUTH
		Pass	1 NT
Pass	2♣	Pass	2♠
Pass	3♠	Pass	4♠
All Pass			

Not every North would have used Stayman (or bid at all) with such weak spades and the doubleton ♣AK. A hand such as 7643,J104,AK72,32 would have been a more attractive 2♣ response. The contract is odds-against; you seem to need two winning finesses plus no unfriendly breaks.

West leads the ♥9. East wins with the king and shifts to the ♦3. How do you play?

****

It is no good putting up an honor. East, who didn't open the bidding, has the ♥AK, and you need him to have the ♠K. He can't have the ♦A. Follow with the ♦6. You must hope the East-West cards are

```
♠ 9 5                    ♠ K 10 8
♥ 9 8 7 3                ♥ A K 5
♦ A 5 4                  ♦ J 10 3
♣ 10 8 6 3               ♣ 9 7 5 2
```

Dlr: West
Vul: E-W

```
              ♠ K J 8 5
              ♥ 5 4 3
              ♦ 9 4 2
              ♣ J 5 2


              ♠ A 9 7 4 2
              ♥ K 6
              ♦ A K 7 5 3
              ♣ 4
```

WEST	NORTH	EAST	SOUTH
1♣	Pass	1♥	1♠
2♣	2♠	3♣	3♦
3♥	3♠	4♥	4♠
All Pass			

After some spirited competitive bidding, you play at 4♠. West leads the ♣K and continues with the ♣A. East follows with the eight and six, and you ruff. At the third trick, you lead a trump to dummy's king, and West plays the ten. On the next trump, East plays low.

Do you put up your ace or finesse with your nine?

****

West's bidding suggests six clubs and three hearts, and he is likely to have the ♥A. You can avoid losing two hearts by setting up your diamonds for heart discards, but only if you lose a diamond trick to West. Therefore, you must hope West has three-card length in diamonds -- so a singleton in spades.

Finesse with the ♠9, hoping the East-West cards resemble

```
    ♠ 10                    ♠ Q 6 3
    ♥ A 9 7                 ♥ Q J 10 8 2
    ♦ Q 10 6                ♦ J 8
    ♣ A K 10 9 7 3          ♣ Q 8 6
```

That was the layout when the deal arose in the 1989 Women's Team Trials, and the late Edith Freilich found the winning play.

```
Dlr: East          ♠ A 5 3
Vul: None          ♥ K 6 5
                   ♦ A J 10 7 5
                   ♣ 8 3


                   ♠ K 4 2
                   ♥ A 3 2
                   ♦ K 8 6 3
                   ♣ A Q 5
```

WEST	NORTH	EAST	SOUTH
		3♣	3 NT
Pass	6 NT	All Pass	

Everybody overbid. South based his 3NT on the expectation that North had some values, but South needed more in the way of playing tricks to contract for nine tricks. North's raise to slam could have been right, but he could have given South a little leeway.

You wouldn't have reached 6NT, but suppose South faints when he sees the dummy. While waiting for the paramedics, East-West ask you to play the hand. West leads the ♣9, and your queen wins.

You cash the ♦K, and East-West follow low. On the next diamond, West plays low. What do you play from dummy?

****

Since East probably has seven clubs to West's one, the odds favor a finesse. But in the context of this deal, you must play the ♦A.

Assuming you pick up the diamonds, your only chance for a 12th trick lies with a major-suit squeeze against West. Even if East can guard one of the majors, a more complex squeeze won't operate since the only way to "rectify the count" is to lose a club, and that would mean losing your threat card in clubs against East. Instead, you must hope that only West guards both majors; hence you must play East for 2-2-2-7 pattern.

```
♠ Q 10 9 8 7        ♠ J 6
♥ Q J 10 9 8        ♥ 7 4
♦ 4 2               ♦ Q 9
♣ 9                 ♣ K J 10 7 6 4 2
```

After you drop the ♦Q, duck a club. Later, West will succumb to the run of your minor-suit winners.

Dlr: West ♠ A J 6 2
Vul: None ♥ J 4
　　　　　 ♦ K 5 2
　　　　　 ♣ K J 8 3

　　　　　 ♠ K Q 10 7 5 3
　　　　　 ♥ K 7 5 3
　　　　　 ♦ 9
　　　　　 ♣ Q 5

WEST	NORTH	EAST	SOUTH
Pass	1♣	Pass	1♠
Dbl	2♠	Pass	4♠
All Pass			

West leads the ♦A and continues with the ♦Q. I'll help you over the first hurdle: You play low from dummy, deferring a discard on the ♦K, and ruff in your hand. Now you can almost certainly make 4♠. See why? How do you continue?

****

Lead a trump to dummy and return a club. If West captures your queen, you will lose one heart, one diamond and one club; East will be marked with the ♥A since West, a passed hand, has shown the ♦AQ and ♣A.

If East has the ♣A, he can't defend effectively. If he plays low, you can win with the queen, draw trumps, discard your last club on the ♦K and ruff out the ♣A, losing two hearts and a diamond. If East grabs his ♣A and leads a diamond, you discard three hearts on the ♦K and ♣KJ, losing one heart, one club and one diamond. If instead East leads a heart, play low, giving West the ♥A for his double and East the ♥Q.

　　　　♠ 8 4　　　　　　　　　　♠ 9
　　　　♥ A 8 6 2　　　　　　　　♥ Q 10 9
　　　　♦ A Q J 8　　　　　　　　♦ 10 7 6 4 3
　　　　♣ 6 4 2　　　　　　　　　♣ A 10 9 7

Dlr: North
Vul: N-S

       ♠ 10 9 7
       ♥ 10 9 6
       ♦ A Q 10 9 2
       ♣ 9 3

       ♠ Q 5 4 2
       ♥ A Q J 4 3 2
       ♦ 7
       ♣ A Q

WEST	NORTH	EAST	SOUTH
	Pass	Pass	1♥
Pass	2♥	Pass	4♥
All Pass			

After 1♥-2♥, some players would bid 4♥ with almost any South hand containing a six-card suit. Here, South has a reasonably sound 4♥ bid.

West leads the ♠K and continues with the three. East takes the ace and returns the ♠J, and West ruffs your queen and leads the ♦8. The defenders are off to a roaring start. How can you salvage the contract? Which finesses will you try?

****

Assume that the trump finesse will work. In that case, it can't be right to rise with the ♦A, planning to finesse in trumps and later in clubs. East didn't open the bidding and has shown the ♠AJ. If he has the ♥K, he can't have both minor-suit kings. If the club finesse works, the diamond finesse would have worked as well; if the diamond finesse loses, the club finesse would have lost also.

Finesse with the ♦Q and lead the ♥10. This will be a winning line of play if East-West have

      ♠ K 3   ♠ A J 8 6
      ♥ 8 7   ♥ K 5
      ♦ K 8 4 3   ♦ J 6 5
      ♣ K 10 8 4 2   ♣ J 7 6 5

An inference is also available from West's defense: If he didn't have the ♦K, he surely would have tried a club at the fourth trick.

```
Dlr: North          ♠ Q 9 6 4
Vul: Both           ♥ A Q
                    ♦ 7
                    ♣ J 7 6 5 3 2


                    ♠ K J 10 8 7
                    ♥ 10 6 3
                    ♦ A J 5
                    ♣ K 4
```

WEST	NORTH	EAST	SOUTH
	Pass	Pass	1♠
Pass	4♠	All Pass	

It looks as if North didn't know how many spades to bid and decided he might as well bid game. West leads a trump, and East takes the ace and shifts to a low diamond, won by your ace. You would like to set up the clubs and avoid the heart finesse. What is your plan of play?

****

If East holds the ♣A, you might make an easy overtrick; but say you lead a trump to dummy and try a club to your king. If West takes the ace and shifts to a heart, you will be in danger of four losers.

Assume that East has the ♥K since if West has it, you are safe. Then your best approach is to lead the ♣4 from your hand at the third trick -- a different sort of "backward finesse." The East-West cards may be

```
♠ 5 3 2                    ♠ A
♥ J 9 5                    ♥ K 8 7 4 2
♦ K 10 6 4                 ♦ Q 9 8 3 2
♣ A 9 8                    ♣ Q 10
```

West can't gain by rising with the ♣A to lead a heart; you would lose only a trump and a club. If he plays low, East wins but can't lead a heart effectively. You will have time to set up and cash the long clubs. (You need not worry about someone having a singleton ♣A. If West had one he would have led it, and East won't have two singleton aces.)

What if East had the ♣A and West had the ♣Q? Then West could take the queen and lead a heart, but you would make your game because the heart finesse would win. If East had both black aces, a diamond honor and the ♥K, he would have opened the bidding.

CHAPTER 3

Through the other's eyes

There is a lovely passage in the works of Henry David Thoreau: "Could a greater miracle take place than for us to look through each other's eyes for an instant?"

Good defense requires forming a picture of declarer's hand. Counting his shape, high-card points and possible winners is vital, and the bidding and play may offer help. But a defender must draw inferences, and to do that, he can look at the deal from declarer's point of view -- through his eyes.

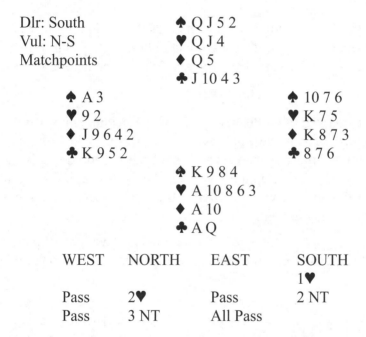

Dlr: South
Vul: N-S
Matchpoints

	♠ Q J 5 2	
	♥ Q J 4	
	♦ Q 5	
	♣ J 10 4 3	
♠ A 3		♠ 10 7 6
♥ 9 2		♥ K 7 5
♦ J 9 6 4 2		♦ K 8 7 3
♣ K 9 5 2		♣ 8 7 6
	♠ K 9 8 4	
	♥ A 10 8 6 3	
	♦ A 10	
	♣ A Q	

WEST	NORTH	EAST	SOUTH
			1♥
Pass	2♥	Pass	2 NT
Pass	3 NT	All Pass	

North-South reached a questionable contract but survived. West led the ♦4, and declarer misguessed by playing the queen from dummy. When East's king covered, South took the ace and led a spade. West rose with the ace and ... returned a spade. South won, picked up the hearts with finesses and cashed all his winners. At the end, he endplayed West with the ♦J to lead from the ♣K. Making five, +660 and a North-South top!

West could have beaten 3NT by laying down his ♦J when he took the ♠A. Clearly, he feared that South had 10-x left. But West should have inferred that South couldn't have the ♦10 unless he had started with the doubleton A-10. If South held A-10-x, he would have played low from dummy on the first diamond to assure a second stopper.

```
Dlr: South          ♠ 10 7 6
Vul: N-S            ♥ K 6 5
                    ♦ K Q 10 6 5
                    ♣ Q 4
   ♠ K J 8 2
   ♥ A 4
   ♦ 8 7
   ♣ J 10 9 8 2
```

WEST	NORTH	EAST	SOUTH
			1 NT
Pass	3 NT	All Pass	

You lead the ♣J, and dummy's queen holds. Next, dummy leads a heart: jack from East (suggesting a sequential holding), queen from declarer. You take the ace and have options. Which one do you choose?

****

Declarer is marked with the ♣AK. (If East has a club honor yet failed to cover dummy's queen, your play is moot; you won't win with this partner.) South had the ♥Q and is sure to have the ♦A and possibly the ♦J also. If he needed to set up the diamonds, he would have done so first thing. Nor would he have won the first club with the queen, which might have been dummy's only entry to the long diamonds.

So declarer cannot have the ♠AQ, which would give him 19 points. Moreover, if he has the ♠A, the contract is unbeatable. Shift to the ♠2.

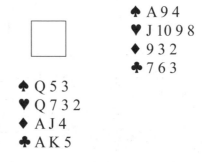

```
                              ♠ A 9 4
                              ♥ J 10 9 8
                              ♦ 9 3 2
                              ♣ 7 6 3
        ♠ Q 5 3
        ♥ Q 7 3 2
        ♦ A J 4
        ♣ A K 5
```

East should take the ♠A and return a spade instead of returning to clubs. He should treat your ♠2 as showing interest in spades. If you wanted him to win and shift back to clubs, you would lead a higher spade.

```
Dlr: South        ♠ A J 8
Vul: N-S          ♥ A 9 7 5 4 2
                  ♦ 6 3
                  ♣ J 5

♠ 7 2
♥ K 10 3          ┌──────┐
♦ 10 8 4          │      │
♣ K Q 10 9 3      └──────┘


WEST    NORTH    EAST      SOUTH
                           1♦
Pass    1♥       Pass      1♠
Pass    2♥       Pass      2 NT
Pass    3 NT     All Pass
```

You lead the ♣Q, conventionally asking East to clarify the position by playing the jack if he has it. (This approach is widely played but not foolproof; once I led the queen from this holding, dummy had x-x, and my partner had A-x-x. He took the ace and shifted, thinking declarer had the king.)

When you see dummy, you know East can't oblige. But when he follows with the deuce, South plays low and also plays low when you continue with the ♣K.

What do you lead at the third trick?

****

If South had minimum values, he would have passed 2♥ in a flash. His bidding promises extra strength -- perhaps 16 or 17 points. But South is marked with A-8-4 in clubs. With 4-2-4-3 pattern, he would have opened 1NT. Play him for a singleton heart. In case it's the queen, shift to the ♥K.

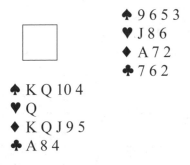

```
                        ♠ 9 6 5 3
     ┌──────┐           ♥ J 8 6
     │      │           ♦ A 7 2
     └──────┘           ♣ 7 6 2

     ♠ K Q 10 4
     ♥ Q
     ♦ K Q J 9 5
     ♣ A 8 4
```

If you plug away at clubs instead, South will win and go after the diamonds. He can set up four tricks there and make an overtrick.

Dlr: North   ♠ K Q 10 5
Vul: N-S   ♥ J 10
Matchpoints   ♦ A K Q 2
                ♣ 7 6 5

♠ A 4
♥ K 4
♦ 10 9 8 4 3
♣ K 10 4 2

WEST	NORTH	EAST	SOUTH
	1♦	Pass	1♥
Pass	1♠	Pass	3♥
Pass	4♥	All Pass	

North's tens improved his hand, but apparently he wasn't willing to open 1NT with two unstopped suits. South's jump-rebid of 3♥ was invitational, not forcing.

You lead the ♣2. Inexperienced players are often terrified of leading from a king, but to lead the unbid suit here is all but mandatory. East plays the jack, and declarer takes the ace. He leads the ♦7 to dummy -- East plays the six -- and lets the ♥J ride to your king.

What do you lead next?

****

Should you try to cash a club? Look through the other's eyes. How would you play as declarer if you had a club loser and only one or two diamonds. Wouldn't you try to discard your loser on dummy's diamonds before you risked the trump finesse? Even if you had two diamonds, the chance of a 4-3 break would be 62 percent.

To try to cash your ♣K can't be right. Declarer doesn't have a club loser unless he also has three diamonds. Lead the ♦10, your highest diamond as a suit-preference play, asking partner to return a spade when he ruffs.

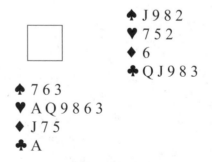

                                   ♠ J 9 8 2
                                   ♥ 7 5 2
                                   ♦ 6
                                   ♣ Q J 9 8 3

                ♠ 7 6 3
                ♥ A Q 9 8 6 3
                ♦ J 7 5
                ♣ A

At IMPs, declarer might have led trumps from his hand. At matchpoints, he gave in to the lure of overtricks.

Dlr: West   ♠ K Q 10 6 5
Vul: Both   ♥ K J 10 6 4
               ♦ K
               ♣ 7 5

♠ 7 2
♥ A 2
♦ Q J 10 6 4
♣ A J 6 4

WEST	NORTH	EAST	SOUTH
1♦	2♦	Pass	3♠
Pass	4♠	All Pass	

North's 2♦ was a Michaels cuebid, showing length in both majors. Most players use the convention to show either a strong hand or a weak, offensively oriented hand. The actual North hand is an in-betweener. Some players might have overcalled 1♠ and bid hearts next. In any case, North thought he was worth game when South invited with 3♠.

You lead the ♦Q. Dummy's king wins, and declarer continues with a heart to his queen and your ace.

What do you lead at the third trick?

****

To try to cash some clubs is tempting; maybe East has the king. But if declarer has the ♠A, why didn't he come to his hand and discard a club from dummy on his ♦A?

The play marks East with the ♠A. Lead a trump and let him win and return a club.

                         ♠ A 8
                         ♥ 8 7 5 3
                         ♦ 8 7 2
                         ♣ Q 9 3 2

♠ J 9 4 3
♥ Q 9
♦ A 9 5 3
♣ K 10 8

Dlr: North   ♠ Q 10 5
Vul: N-S   ♥ A K Q 10 7 6
              ♦ 10 5
              ♣ 10 4

                              ♠ A J 9 2
                              ♥ 5 4
                              ♦ A 8 4 2
                              ♣ K 9 3

WEST	NORTH	EAST	SOUTH
	1♥	Dbl	Redbl
2♣	2♥	Pass	3 NT
All Pass			

After South's strength-showing redouble, North's free rebid of 2♥ suggests a minimum hand. With a stronger hand, North could mark time by passing over West's run-out to 2♣. South leaped to 3NT anyway.

West leads the ♣5: ten, king, ace. South then leads the ♥8 to dummy and returns the ♦10. How do you defend?

$$********$$

Surely South has the ♣Q. With A-x-x he would have held up his ace. With A-J-x he would have played low from dummy on the first club to assure a second stopper.

So South has eight tricks, and a diamond trick will make nine. If South holds the K-J, he will not misguess after your double. What about rising with the ♦A to continue clubs, playing West for the ♦K? If declarer's diamonds are no better than Q-J-x-x, he must hold the ♠K for his bid, and then he would have forced out the ♠A for nine tricks.

Your only chance is to play West for the ♠K. Grab your ♦A and lead a low spade.

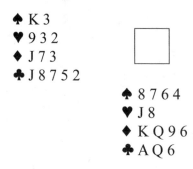

      ♠ K 3
      ♥ 9 3 2
      ♦ J 7 3
      ♣ J 8 7 5 2

               ♠ 8 7 6 4
               ♥ J 8
               ♦ K Q 9 6
               ♣ A Q 6

Dlr: South   ♠ J 4
Vul: N-S   ♥ Q 7 4 3
                  ♦ Q 8 6
                  ♣ K Q 10 5

♠ K 10 8 3
♥ 8 6
♦ K J 7 4
♣ A 9 3

WEST	NORTH	EAST	SOUTH
			1♥
Dbl	Redbl	Pass	Pass
1♠	2♥	Pass	4♥
All Pass			

Your takeout double looks hungry to me, but maybe you adhere to a style in which favorable vulnerability gives you license to overstate your values.

You lead a trump, and declarer takes the A-K and leads the ♣J. You take your ace, and East signals "count" with the eight. What do you lead next?

****

If East had only two clubs, he would have had a five-card or longer suit and would have bid it over the redouble. (That action would imply no values, only a possible place to play.) So declarer has only two clubs and is about to discard on dummy's good clubs. To have a chance, you must cash some winners. Should you try spades or diamonds?

Your double suggested good support for the other major, and if East had four cards in spades, his duty would have been to try 1♠ over the redouble. Since he did not, you can place South with four spades. Two spade discards on the clubs won't help him, but if East has the ♦A, you must take your diamond tricks. Lead the ♦K and continue with the jack.

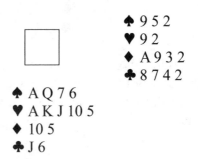

                         ♠ 9 5 2
                         ♥ 9 2
                         ♦ A 9 3 2
                         ♣ 8 7 4 2

♠ A Q 7 6
♥ A K J 10 5
♦ 10 5
♣ J 6

If you take two diamonds (without setting up dummy's queen in the process), your ♠K will score for down one.

```
Dlr: South          ♠ 8 5
Vul: N-S            ♥ J 9 8 3
                    ♦ A K 4 3
                    ♣ K 7 2
                                        ♠ 10 9 7 6 3
                                        ♥ Q 10 6 2
                                        ♦ 8 6
                                        ♣ A 3
```

WEST	NORTH	EAST	SOUTH
			1 NT
Pass	2♣	Pass	2♠
Pass	3 NT	All Pass	

West leads the ♣4, and dummy plays low. You take your ace, and South follows with the five.

What do you return?

****

The bidding tells you that West has at most a doubleton spade, and he led from a four-card club suit. If he had five diamonds, he would have led a diamond; hence his pattern should be 2-3-4-4, leaving South with 4-2-3-4. You should shift to a heart.

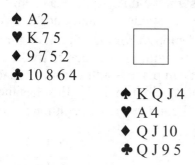

```
♠ A 2
♥ K 7 5
♦ 9 7 5 2
♣ 10 8 6 4
                    ♠ K Q J 4
                    ♥ A 4
                    ♦ Q J 10
                    ♣ Q J 9 5
```

If South plays low, West takes the king and returns a heart, which you duck to South's ace. South has only eight winners, and when West gets in with the ♠A, a third heart lead through dummy's J-9 to your Q-10 will sink the contract.

Dlr: South
Vul: N-S

♠ A Q 5
♥ 5 3
♦ A Q 9
♣ 10 8 7 5 4

♠ J 3
♥ K 9 4
♦ K 5 4 3
♣ Q J 9 2

WEST	NORTH	EAST	SOUTH
			1♦
Pass	2♣	Pass	2 NT
Pass	3 NT	All Pass	

West leads the ♥2. South takes your king with the ace and leads the ♦10. West follows with the eight, South lets the ten ride and you take your king.

What do you return?

****

West had four hearts and no more than four spades, else his opening lead would have been a spade. It's possible that South opened 1♦ with 4-4-3-2 pattern, but not after West signalled with the eight on the first diamond. Probably, South's shape is 4-4-4-1, so you should shift to the ♣2. You will punish North-South's aggressive bidding if the West and South hands are

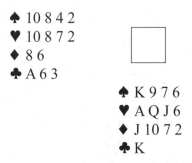

♠ 10 8 4 2
♥ 10 8 7 2
♦ 8 6
♣ A 6 3

♠ K 9 7 6
♥ A Q J 6
♦ J 10 7 2
♣ K

Even if South happened to hold one more club and one fewer diamond, your club shift would probably beat 3NT.

Dlr: North   ♠ 10 5 2
Vul: None   ♥ K J 8 5 2
                  ♦ A Q
                  ♣ K Q J
                              ♠ A 9 8 7 6 4 3
                              ♥ 6
                              ♦ 2
                              ♣ 9 4 3 2

WEST   NORTH   EAST   SOUTH
         1 NT   Pass   6♥
All Pass

South appears to have won his gamble when dummy hits with spectacular trump support. West leads the ♠Q, and when you play the ace, South follows with the king.

If West has the ♣A, you may need to cash it now; if declarer's ♠K was a singleton, he can set up a winner with dummy's ten and obtain a club discard. But if West's ♠Q was a singleton, you had better give him a ruff.

What's your poison?

****

People who bid as South did aren't worried about missing aces. If South had a hand such as K,AQ10973,KJ1053,5, he would have stopped off for an ace-asking bid. On the actual auction, South is a heavy favorite to be void in clubs. Return a spade.

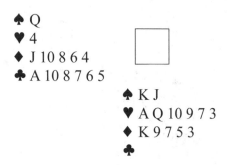

♠ Q
♥ 4
♦ J 10 8 6 4
♣ A 10 8 7 6 5

              ♠ K J
              ♥ A Q 10 9 7 3
              ♦ K 9 7 5 3
              ♣

```
Dlr: South          ♠ Q 6 2
Vul: N-S            ♥ K 7
                    ♦ K Q 10 9 4
                    ♣ J 6 3
    ♠ K 10
    ♥ Q J 10 9 4        _____
    ♦ 8 7 5 2          |        |
    ♣ Q 10             |_____|
```

WEST	NORTH	EAST	SOUTH
			1♣
Pass	1♦	Pass	1 NT
Pass	3 NT	All Pass	

You lead the ♥Q, and South wins with dummy's king and leads a spade: three, jack. king.

It's your play to the third trick.

****

Declarer should have the ♠A. On the bidding, he has at most three spades, and he wouldn't lead a spade with J-x-x; he might lose five fast spade tricks.

South also has the ♦A, else he would have won the first heart in his hand, saving dummy's king as a certain entry, and attacked the diamonds. So you can give South 13 HCP, which means he doesn't have a high club. Shift to the ♣Q and another club despite South's opening bid.

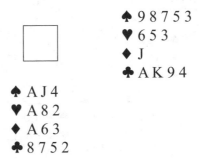

```
                        ♠ 9 8 7 5 3
     _____           ♥ 6 5 3
    |        |          ♦ J
    |_____|          ♣ A K 9 4
    ♠ A J 4
    ♥ A 8 2
    ♦ A 6 3
    ♣ 8 7 5 2
```

If you fail to shift, South will take five diamonds, two hearts and two spades.

```
Dlr: South        ♠ K Q
Vul: Both         ♥ K 10 4
                  ♦ 10 8 5 2
                  ♣ K Q J 2
                                    ♠ 9 7 6 3
                                    ♥ Q 7 2
                                    ♦ Q 7 6 4
                                    ♣ A 6
```

WEST	NORTH	EAST	SOUTH
			1♥
Pass	2♣	Pass	2 NT
Pass	3♥	Pass	4♥
All Pass			

South's bid of 2NT suggested near-minimum values. West leads the ♠2, and declarer overtakes dummy's queen with his ace and leads the ♥9: six, four, queen.

How do you defend?

****

Declarer appears to lack the ♥A. If he had it, he would have no reason to win the first trick in his hand, and he might have cashed the ace (or cashed the king) before trying a finesse.

Then South is marked with the ♦AK. Your best chance is to shift to the ♣A and a low club, hoping West can give you a third-round club ruff when he takes the ♥A.

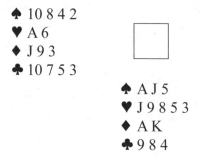

```
♠ 10 8 4 2
♥ A 6
♦ J 9 3
♣ 10 7 5 3
                    ♠ A J 5
                    ♥ J 9 8 5 3
                    ♦ A K
                    ♣ 9 8 4
```

If South's hand were AJ5,J9853,AK3,98, he could and probably would still make 4♥ if you shifted to a low diamond at trick three.

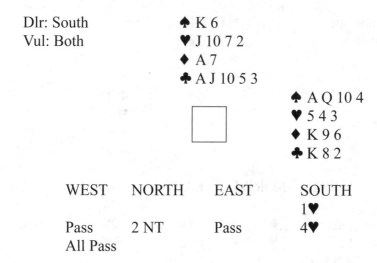

Dlr: South
Vul: Both

♠ K 6
♥ J 10 7 2
♦ A 7
♣ A J 10 5 3

♠ A Q 10 4
♥ 5 4 3
♦ K 9 6
♣ K 8 2

WEST	NORTH	EAST	SOUTH
			1♥
Pass	2 NT	Pass	4♥
All Pass			

After North's 2NT -- a conventional forcing heart raise -- South's jump to 4♥ says he wants to play there.

West leads the ♠2, and South puts up dummy's king. After you take the ace, what do you lead at the second trick?

****

This is not difficult. Return the ♠4. West has the ♠J. If South had the jack, he would have played low from dummy on the first spade, hoping West led from the queen.

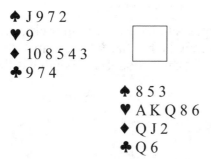

♠ J 9 7 2
♥ 9
♦ 10 8 5 4 3
♣ 9 7 4

♠ 8 5 3
♥ A K Q 8 6
♦ Q J 2
♣ Q 6

West will win and shift to a diamond, assuring the defense of four tricks.

Declarer made a serious error when he played the ♠K. If he plays low, the defense can get only two spades and a club.

Dlr: South   ♠ Q 7 4
Vul: N-S   ♥ J 10 8 2
              ♦ K 5 4 3
              ♣ 8 3

                             ♠ J 9 3 2
                             ♥ 4
                             ♦ A 8 6 2
                             ♣ J 9 7 4

WEST	NORTH	EAST	SOUTH
			2♣
Pass	2♦	Pass	2♥
Pass	3♥	Pass	6♥
All Pass			

West leads the ♣2: three, jack, king. Declarer leads a low trump to dummy's jack and returns a low diamond. Do you rise with your ace or play low?

****

Play low. If declarer had the singleton queen, West's opening lead would have been the ♦J from J-10-9-7, not a club from a broken suit.

South wins with the queen, and West follows with the seven. South goes back to dummy with the ♥10 (West plays the nine) and leads a second low diamond. Do you put up the ace this time?

****

Play low again. South appears to have six trump tricks, plus the ♣AK and a club ruff in dummy. Surely he has the ♠A; he leaped to slam without checking on missing aces with Blackwood. So if South has the ♦QJ, he has 12 tricks.

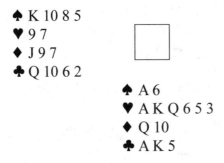

     ♠ K 10 8 5
     ♥ 9 7
     ♦ J 9 7
     ♣ Q 10 6 2

                     ♠ A 6
                     ♥ A K Q 6 5 3
                     ♦ Q 10
                     ♣ A K 5

Proper defense will net East-West a spade trick as well as a diamond.

Declarer could have tried a finesse with the ♦10 for his 12th trick. His psychological approach might succeed if East failed to count.

Dlr: South   ♠ 6 5 3
Vul: Both   ♥ J 8 3
                  ♦ 6 4
                  ♣ A Q 10 7 2

♠ J 9 8 2
♥ A 6 2
♦ J 9 5
♣ 8 4 3

WEST	NORTH	EAST	SOUTH
			1♥
Pass	2♥	Pass	4♥
All Pass			

Without conviction, you lead a trump against South's game. East produces the king and returns a trump to your ace. The defense may have started well, but dummy's clubs look menacing. What do you lead at the third trick?

****

Look through your partner's eyes. Unless he knew dummy's club suit would be no threat, he would not have led a second trump. He would have shifted, probably to a spade, perhaps to a diamond, to try to build a trick before declarer drew trumps and used the clubs.

You should follow partner's defense; lead a third trump.

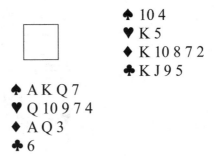

                        ♠ 10 4
                        ♥ K 5
                        ♦ K 10 8 7 2
                        ♣ K J 9 5

♠ A K Q 7
♥ Q 10 9 7 4
♦ A Q 3
♣ 6

Declarer succeeds with any other defense. He can ruff a loser in dummy.

Dlr: South   ♠ A J
Vul: None   ♥ Q 9 4 3
                 ♦ K Q 3
                 ♣ Q 7 5 3

♠ 6 5
♥ K 5
♦ 7 6 5 4
♣ J 10 9 4 2

WEST	NORTH	EAST	SOUTH
			1♠
Pass	2 NT	Pass	3♥
Pass	4♥	Pass	4 NT
Pass	5♦	Pass	6♥
All Pass			

North-South play a 2NT response as natural and forcing.

Against South's slam, you lead the ♣J, covered by the queen, king and ace. Declarer leads a spade to dummy's ace and passes the ♥Q to your king.

What do you lead at the third trick?

****

If you "cashed" a club, declarer guffaws as he ruffs, draws trumps and runs the spades to discard dummy's diamonds. The missing hands are

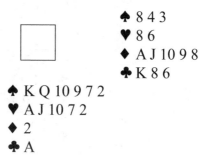

                        ♠ 8 4 3
                        ♥ 8 6
                        ♦ A J 10 9 8
                        ♣ K 8 6

♠ K Q 10 9 7 2
♥ A J 10 7 2
♦ 2
♣ A

If South had a club loser, he would also lack the ♦A. If he had KQ1097,AJ107,A2,A6, he would have pitched his last club on the diamonds before taking the trump finesse.

What if South held KQ10972,AJ1072,Void,A6? Then he wouldn't have used Blackwood. He would have tried for slam with a 5♣ cuebid.

CHAPTER 4

Counting as declarer

"There are only three kinds of people: those who can count, and those who can't." -- Anonymous

I'll amend that silly quote: There are four kinds of bridge players: those who can count, those who can't, and those who can but don't because they believe the process is arcane and inaccessible.

Counting the distribution of the concealed hands is simple in principle. Anyone can do it with practice and focus. Each hand and each suit have 13 cards. If your opponent started with six clubs, two diamonds and two hearts, he had three spades. If you had six clubs, dummy had one and your left-hand opponent showed up with three, your right-hand opponent had no more than three.

Counting won't be required at every contract you declare, but at some contracts it will be essential.

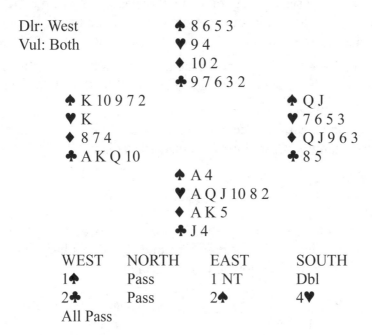

```
Dlr: West            ♠ 8 6 5 3
Vul: Both            ♥ 9 4
                     ♦ 10 2
                     ♣ 9 7 6 3 2
    ♠ K 10 9 7 2              ♠ Q J
    ♥ K                       ♥ 7 6 5 3
    ♦ 8 7 4                   ♦ Q J 9 6 3
    ♣ A K Q 10                ♣ 8 5
                     ♠ A 4
                     ♥ A Q J 10 8 2
                     ♦ A K 5
                     ♣ J 4
```

WEST	NORTH	EAST	SOUTH
1♠	Pass	1 NT	Dbl
2♣	Pass	2♠	4♥
All Pass			

West cashes two high clubs and leads a third. South ruffs, takes the ♦AK and ruffs his last diamond in dummy. He leads the ♥9 next, and East plays low.

On the bidding, South knows that West had five or six spades. He had four clubs and three diamonds, hence one heart at most. To let the ♥9 ride can't gain; if East has K-x-x-x, he is always due a trump trick. South should put up the ♥A in case West has the singleton king.

Dlr: South
Vul: N-S

```
                          ♠ K 9 5 3
                          ♥ K J 8 4
                          ♦ 8 7
                          ♣ A Q 6


                          ♠ A Q J 8 4
                          ♥ A 9 5 2
                          ♦ Q 2
                          ♣ 8 4
```

WEST	NORTH	EAST	SOUTH
			1♠
2♦	3♦	Pass	4♠
All Pass			

North's 3♦ cuebid showed a good hand with spade support but did not promise a diamond control. With one more club and one fewer diamond, North could have jumped to 4♠.

West cashes the ♦KA, East playing the three and six. West shifts to the ♣J. You finesse with the queen, losing to East, alas. A club comes back to West's ten and dummy's ace.

You draw trumps with the ace, queen and king, finding East with three. When you ruff dummy's last club, West discards a diamond.

How do you play the hearts?

****

West had two clubs, one trump and no more than six diamonds (since East signaled low-high on West's high diamonds). So West had four hearts. Cash the ace and lead low to dummy's eight.

```
      ♠ 2                        ♠ 10 7 6
      ♥ Q 10 7 6                 ♥ 3
      ♦ A K J 9 5 4             ♦ 10 6 3
      ♣ J 10                    ♣ K 9 7 5 3 2
```

Dlr: West		♠ 8 7 3	
Vul: Both		♥ K 8 7 4 3	
		♦ A K J	
		♣ A K	

♠ J 4
♥ A J 6 5 2
♦ 10 4 3
♣ J 6 5

WEST	NORTH	EAST	SOUTH
1♠	Dbl	Pass	2♥
Pass	3♥	Pass	4♥
All Pass			

West takes the ♠KQ and continues with the ace. East follows. You ruff and lead a trump to dummy's king; East annoys you by discarding a club. You cash the ♣AK, come to your ♥A and ruff your ♣J in dummy as West's queen covers.

How do you continue?

****

West had five spades, three hearts and at least three clubs, so two diamonds at most. You need not plan to finesse in diamonds. Take the ♦AK. If West follows with low diamonds, exit with a trump, and he will have to concede a ruff-sluff.

♠ A K Q 9 5		♠ 10 6 2
♥ Q 10 9		♥ —
♦ 7 6		♦ Q 9 8 5 2
♣ Q 9 4		♣ 10 8 7 3 2

```
Dlr: North          ♠ A 8 4 2
Vul: None           ♥ Q 9 8
                    ♦ 10 5 2
                    ♣ Q 8 3


                    ♠ 7 5
                    ♥ A J 10 7 4 2
                    ♦ A K J 4
                    ♣ 6
```

WEST	NORTH	EAST	SOUTH
	Pass	3♣	3♥
Pass	4♥	All Pass	

North must like the way you play 'em. Since his ♣Q was a wasted honor, his raise to 4♥ was questionable. West leads the ♠K, and you take dummy's ace and let the ♥9 ride. West wins and cashes the ♠Q, and East, who followed with the ten on the first spade, discards a high club.

West shifts to the ♣J, winning, and leads a second club, You ruff East's nine, lead a trump to dummy -- East shows out -- and ruff the last club, West discarding a spade. You cash the ♦A (three from West, six from East), draw West's trump with the queen and lead a second diamond from dummy. East plays the seven.

Do you finesse?

****

You have a complete count. East started with one spade, one heart and seven clubs, so four diamonds. Even if you win a finesse with the jack, you will still lose a diamond to East. Put up the ♦K, hoping West had Q-x.

```
♠ K Q J 9 6 3           ♠ 10
♥ K 5 3                 ♥ 6
♦ Q 3                   ♦ 9 8 7 6
♣ J 4                   ♣ A K 10 9 7 5 2
```

Unless you count the hands, your chances of making this contract dwindle.

```
Dlr: South          ♠ A K 4
Vul: Both           ♥ Q J 7 5
                    ♦ 9 6 2
                    ♣ Q 6 2


                    ♠ 6 2
                    ♥ A K 10 9
                    ♦ Q 8 5
                    ♣ K J 5 3
```

WEST	NORTH	EAST	SOUTH
			1♣
1♠	Dbl	Pass	2♥
Pass	4♥	All Pass	

North's double was negative, suggesting heart length but too few hearts or too little strength for a bid of 2♥. South's 2♥ was not a reverse; he was only "raising" the suit North implied.

West leads the ♦K. (They lead the king from A-K-x.) East signals with the three, so West shifts to the ♠J. You win and draw trumps, finding West with three.

How do you play the clubs?

****

West, who overcalled vulnerable, surely has the ♣A. East could have raised to 2♠ with ♠Qxx and the ♣A. But West is marked with three diamonds; with the doubleton A-K, he would have led the ace.

Lead a club to the queen, intending to play low on the way back. If your picture of the deal is correct, West's ace will fall, and you can pitch a diamond from dummy on the ♣KJ, losing one club and two diamonds.

```
        ♠ J 10 9 5 3          ♠ Q 8 7
        ♥ 8 4 3               ♥ 6 2
        ♦ A K J               ♦ 10 7 4 3
        ♣ A 7                 ♣ 10 9 8 4
```

```
Dlr: West          ♠ A
Vul: Both          ♥ A J 4 2
                   ♦ K 8 7 2
                   ♣ K Q 8 3


                   ♠ 9 3
                   ♥ K 9 8 6 3
                   ♦ Q 5 4 3
                   ♣ 5 2
```

WEST	NORTH	EAST	SOUTH
3♠	Dbl	Pass	4♥
All Pass			

West leads the ♣10 to the king and ace. East returns the ♣6 to the five, nine and queen. You take the ♥AK, and West follows once, then discards a spade. You go to the ♠A and ruff a club, and both defenders follow suit.

How do you attack the diamonds?

****

To lose only one diamond, you must hope a defender has A-x. You can lead low through him and duck on the next diamond -- an "obligatory finesse."

West has followed to three clubs and one trump, and you expect him to have seven spades for his vulnerable preempt. (It's possible East might have raised to 4♠ if he had four-card support.) Play West for 7-1-2-3 pattern; start with a diamond to dummy's king.

```
♠ K J 10 8 7 4 2        ♠ Q 6 5
♥ 5                     ♥ Q 10 7
♦ A 6                   ♦ J 10 9
♣ 10 9 4                ♣ A J 7 6
```

True, players who preempt don't usually have side aces, but if East has, say, A-J-9, you have no legitimate play for your contract.

Against a declarer of your caliber, East should have saved at 4♠ -- down one at worst.

```
Dlr: West          ♠ 10 9 7 4
Vul: E-W           ♥ A K 10 7 5 2
                   ♦ 5
                   ♣ 8 4


                   ♠ A Q J 6 2
                   ♥ Q 6
                   ♦ 7 4
                   ♣ Q 10 9 2
```

WEST	NORTH	EAST	SOUTH
1♦	1♥	2♣	2♠
3♦	3♠	4♦	4♠
5♦	5♠	Dbl	All Pass

North's push to 5♠ was by no means obvious; he had promising defense against West's 5♦. But on freakish deals, it often pays to buy the contract.

Against your 5♠ doubled, West leads the ♦K and continues with the ♦A, forcing dummy to ruff. East plays the three and ten. You pass the ♠10 hopefully, but West takes the king and returns a trump. East follows, and you win.

How do you play the hearts?

****

West had two trumps and probably had a seven-card diamond suit. Certainly he had no more than seven since East supported the diamonds. When West got in with the ♠K, why didn't he lead a club for East to take the setting tricks? Clearly, West didn't have a club to lead!

Cash the ♥Q and lead a heart to dummy's ten, playing West for 2-4-7-0 distribution.

```
        ♠ K 5                    ♠ 8 3
        ♥ J 9 8 4                ♥ 3
        ♦ A K Q J 8 6 2          ♦ 10 9 3
        ♣                        ♣ A K J 7 6 5 3
```

You can pitch all four of your clubs on the hearts and score up the contract.

North's "sacrifice" was well judged, as it happened; 5♦ by East-West is cold. Next time, West's opening lead against 5♠ doubled will be the ♦2.

```
Dlr: South          ♠ Q 8
Vul: N-S            ♥ 7 6 2
                    ♦ A 7 5 2
                    ♣ A 10 5 3


                    ♠ 10 7 5
                    ♥ A K
                    ♦ K Q 4 3
                    ♣ K Q 8 2
```

WEST	NORTH	EAST	SOUTH
			1 NT
Pass	3 NT	All Pass	

Against 3NT, West leads the ♠4. You put up dummy's queen, and when East's king covers, you wonder how you could have arranged the auction to end at five of a minor. But after East cashes the ♠J, he ... shifts to the ♥10.

Granted a reprieve, you win with the king and cash the ♦KQ. East discards a heart. When you take the ♥A, West follows with the jack.

How do you play the clubs?

****

West had four diamonds and obviously six spades. He followed to two hearts, so he had one club at most. Lead a club to dummy's ace. If East-West follow low, lead the ♣10 and pass it.

```
♠ A 9 6 4 3 2          ♠ K J
♥ J 8                  ♥ Q 10 9 5 4 3
♦ J 9 8 6              ♦ 10
♣ 7                    ♣ J 9 6 4
```

If East covers the ♣10, you can return to dummy with the ♦A to pick up the clubs, winning four clubs, three diamonds and two hearts.

Dlr: South
Vul: N-S

♠ A J 4 2
♥ Q 4
♦ K 7 5 2
♣ Q 6 4

♠ Q 5 3
♥ K 7
♦ A J 4 3
♣ A K 10 3

WEST	NORTH	EAST	SOUTH
			1 NT
Pass	3 NT	All Pass	

You declare yet another notrump game, and West leads the ♥J. When you play the queen from dummy, East takes the ace and returns the three to your king. You lead a diamond to the king and return a diamond, but when East discards the ♣6, you hastily take the ace.

Next you try a spade to dummy's jack. You need at least two spade tricks. West plays the eight, East the seven. Then both defenders follow low to the ♠A.

How do you play the clubs?

****

West had three spades and four diamonds. It appears from East's fourth-highest return of the ♥3 that West had at least four hearts, so no more than two clubs. Take the ♣AQ and, if the jack hasn't appeared, finesse with the ten next.

♠ K 10 8
♥ J 10 8 5
♦ Q 9 8 6
♣ 9 7

♠ 9 7 6
♥ A 9 6 3 2
♦ 10
♣ J 8 5 2

Dlr: East
Vul: N-S

♠ J 7 6 2
♥ A K 10
♦ K Q J
♣ A Q J

♠ Q 10 9 8 5 3
♥ 7 6 5
♦ 7 6 2
♣ 3

WEST	NORTH	EAST	SOUTH
		1♣	Pass
Pass	Dbl	Pass	1♠
Pass	4♠	All Pass	

West leads the ♦10, and East takes the ace. He cashes the ♠AK -- West discards a club -- and exits with the ♥Q. You take dummy's ace and cash two diamonds. Both defenders follow low and also follow low to the ♥K.

How do you play the clubs to get a discard for your losing heart?

****

Count high-card points. East has shown the ♠AK, ♥QJ and ♦A for a total of 14. East also appears to have balanced pattern: He had two spades, three or four diamonds and three or four hearts. If East had the ♣K, he would have opened 1NT.

Come to your hand and lead a club to the jack.

♠ 4   ♠ A K
♥ 8 4 2   ♥ Q J 9 3
♦ 10 9 8 5   ♦ A 4 3
♣ K 9 8 4 2 ♣ 10 7 6 5

Dlr: South   ♠ K 6
Vul: None   ♥ K J 4
                    ♦ 9 6 3
                    ♣ A 8 5 4 3

                    ♠ Q 8
                    ♥ A Q 10 7 2
                    ♦ K 10
                    ♣ Q J 7 2

WEST	NORTH	EAST	SOUTH
			1♥
3♠	4♥	All Pass	

If there had been no interference, North would have invited game: In "Standard" methods, he would have temporized with a 2♣ response, then supported the hearts. West's preempt forced North to stretch slightly to compete. Anyway, his ♠K looked like a working card.

West leads the ♦J, and East takes the ace and returns a diamond. West ruffs your king, cashes the ♠A and leads another spade. Dummy's king wins; East signals with the ten and deuce. When you draw trumps, you find that West started with four; East had a singleton.

How do you play the clubs?

****

West had seven spades, four hearts and one diamond, hence one club. Lead the ♣2. You must hope West's singleton is the king. Leading an honor will cost the contract if the East-West cards are

♠ A J 9 7 5 4 3   ♠ 10 2
♥ 9 6 5 3   ♥ 8
♦ J   ♦ A Q 8 7 5 4 2
♣ K   ♣ 10 9 6

```
Dlr: South          ♠ Q 9 7 5
Vul: N-S            ♥ K J 3
                    ♦ A K Q 5
                    ♣ 7 3


                    ♠ A K J 3 2
                    ♥ 10 9 7 5
                    ♦ 4
                    ♣ A K 8
```

WEST	NORTH	EAST	SOUTH
			1♠
Pass	2 NT	Pass	3♦
Pass	4♦	Pass	5♣
Pass	6♠	All Pass	

North's 2NT was a conventional forcing raise. Your 3♦ rebid promised a singleton diamond. When you cuebid 5♣ next, North thought he could bid slam since he had a sound hand and a control in hearts.

West leads the ♣5, and you take the ace and draw trumps in two rounds. You cash the ♣K and ruff your last club in dummy, and East discards a heart. Next you take the top diamonds, discarding two hearts. East-West follow suit. When you lead dummy's last diamond, preparing to ruff in your hand to make a heart play, East discards another heart.

How do you proceed?

****

Count the hands. West had two spades, five diamonds, six clubs ... so no hearts. If you ruff that fourth diamond and lead a heart, you will go down for sure. Instead, discard another heart, letting West win. He will have to return a minor-suit card, and you will ruff in dummy and discard your last heart.

```
♠ 10 4                      ♠ 8 6
♥                           ♥ A Q 8 6 4 2
♦ 10 8 7 6 3                ♦ J 9 2
♣ J 9 6 5 4 2               ♣ Q 10
```

```
Dlr: South              ♠ J 5 3
Vul: Both               ♥ A Q 10
                        ♦ A Q 4
                        ♣ Q J 5 3


                        ♠ A Q 4 2
                        ♥ K J
                        ♦ K 5 3 2
                        ♣ A 10 2
```

WEST	NORTH	EAST	SOUTH
			1 NT
Pass	6 NT	All Pass	

North's commitment to slam with three queens and two jacks was a bit optimistic, but secondary values are improved when aces and kings to "put pants on them" are known to lie in the opposite hand. Since you have a 17-point maximum, you would have accepted an invitation.

West leads the ♥9. You win in dummy and pass the ♣Q, winning. A club to the ten also wins, but West discards a heart.

How do you continue?

****

Since East has five clubs to West's one, the odds favor West to hold greater length in spades -- and therefore any particular spade including the king. An inference is also available: If West had weak spades as well as weak hearts, his opening lead might have been a spade.

Try a spade toward dummy's jack. If it wins, you are up to 11 tricks and have chances for one more. Take the ♣A, forcing another discard from West. If he pitches a second heart, you might visualize the East-West cards as

```
♠ K 10 8 7          ♠ 9 6
♥ 9 8 7 5           ♥ 6 4 3 2
♦ J 8 7 6           ♦ 10 9
♣ 7                 ♣ K 9 8 6 4
```

You can cash two more hearts, forcing West to let go a spade, and then three high diamonds. When East discards, you exit with the fourth diamond, and West must return a spade to your A-Q, yielding the contract.

```
Dlr: West          ♠ Q 9 8
Vul: Both          ♥ Q 10 6 3 2
                   ♦ J 6 3
                   ♣ 8 5


                   ♠ A K J 10 5 2
                   ♥ 7
                   ♦ K Q 5 4
                   ♣ K 2
```

WEST	NORTH	EAST	SOUTH
1♣	Pass	1 NT	Dbl
2♣	2♥	3♣	3♠
All Pass			

Since South would have intervened with 2♠ on a weaker hand, he doubled at his first turn to show strength.

West leads the ♦7, and when dummy plays low, East puts on the eight. You take the king and cash the ♠A. All follow low.

You seem to be off two clubs, a heart and a diamond and must also worry about your fourth diamond. How do you continue?

****

West rebid his clubs, East supported: Clubs are 6-3. Since East didn't respond 1♥, hearts are 4-3. East presumably has four diamonds. If he had five, he might have responded 1♦ and could have given West a diamond ruff.

Play West for 1-4-2-6 pattern. At the third trick, lead a diamond to dummy's jack.

```
♠ 4                    ♠ 7 6 3
♥ A K 8 4              ♥ J 9 5
♦ 7 2                  ♦ A 10 9 8
♣ A 10 9 7 6 3        ♣ Q J 4
```

East will take the ace and lead a second trump, but you can win, cash the ♦Q and ruff your fourth diamond in dummy to assure nine tricks.

Tom Sanders found the winning play in a 1983 Spingold match.

Dlr: West   ♠ 7 5
Vul: Both   ♥ K J 10 9 3
             ♦ 8 6 4
             ♣ A 6 4

             ♠ A K 10 8 3 2
             ♥ A Q
             ♦ K 7
             ♣ 9 7 3

WEST	NORTH	EAST	SOUTH
Pass	Pass	3♦	3♠
Pass	4♠	All Pass	

West leads the ♦J, and East takes the ace and, as you fear, returns a diamond for West to ruff. West shifts to the ♣Q, and when you take dummy's ace, East drops the king. You cash the ♠AK, and things get no better when West discards on the second round; East has a trump trick.

How do you continue?

****

East started with three spades, seven diamonds and at least one club, hence no more than two hearts. You cannot make the contract by immediately trying to run the hearts for club discards. East will ruff before you get rid of all your clubs.

Your only hope is to give East his trump trick, assuming he has no more clubs.

     ♠ 9 6   ♠ Q J 4
     ♥ 8 7 6 5   ♥ 4 2
     ♦ J   ♦ A Q 10 9 5 3 2
     ♣ Q J 10 8 5 2   ♣ K

You can ruff East's diamond return and run the hearts in peace.

I suspect most Easts would have opened 1♦.

```
Dlr: South          ♠ Q 6 4
Vul: N-S            ♥ A J 8 3
                    ♦ A 10 8 2
                    ♣ K 6


                    ♠ A J 10
                    ♥ Q 10 9 2
                    ♦ Q J 9 3
                    ♣ A Q
```

WEST	NORTH	EAST	SOUTH
			1 NT
Pass	3 NT	All Pass	

West leads the ♣2. Your partner tables a powerful hand, so you'll have some explaining to do if you fail to produce nine tricks.

Suppose you take the ♣K and give yourself an extra chance by leading the ♠Q. If East has the king and covers, you will be sure of three spades, two clubs, at least three tricks in one red suit, and the ace of the other red suit.

East actually plays low on the ♠Q, so you put up your ace, intending to finesse in both red suits. You will make the contract if either finesse wins. But lo and behold, West drops the ♠K under your ace!

Your contract is now secure, but what about overtricks?

****

West led from a weak four-card club suit. If he had five cards in either red suit, he would have led it. In fact, if West had K-x-x-x in a red suit, he would have preferred to lead that suit.

Lead the ♥Q but play dummy's ace if West follows low.

```
♠ K                      ♠ 9 8 7 5 3 2
♥ 7 6 5 4                ♥ K
♦ 7 6 5 4                ♦ K
♣ 10 7 4 2               ♣ J 9 8 5 3
```

Later, you will drop the singleton ♦K also. Your opponents will mutter about your luck, but your partner will be pleased.

CHAPTER 5

Inferences as declarer

"A cast-iron alibi for going wrong." -- Cy the Cynic, one of the characters in my syndicated column, when asked to define an inference.

Many play assumptions are no more than wishful thinking. Players make them because the alternative is to concede defeat. But some -- called inferences -- are backed up by information or logical reasoning. Inferring the lie of the cards from the bidding and play is the essence of the problem-solving nature of the game.

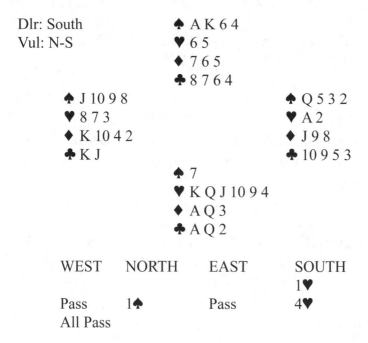

```
Dlr: South          ♠ A K 6 4
Vul: N-S            ♥ 6 5
                    ♦ 7 6 5
                    ♣ 8 7 6 4
   ♠ J 10 9 8                    ♠ Q 5 3 2
   ♥ 8 7 3                       ♥ A 2
   ♦ K 10 4 2                    ♦ J 9 8
   ♣ K J                         ♣ 10 9 5 3
                    ♠ 7
                    ♥ K Q J 10 9 4
                    ♦ A Q 3
                    ♣ A Q 2
```

WEST	NORTH	EAST	SOUTH
			1♥
Pass	1♠	Pass	4♥
All Pass			

West leads the ♠J against 4♥. Declarer takes the A-K to discard a diamond and next tries a diamond to his queen. West takes the king and forces South to ruff a spade. The ♥K goes to East's ace, and he returns ... the ♣3.

Declarer should be wary. East surely had a safe exit in spades or trumps. Dummy has no more entries. If East had the ♣K, he wouldn't offer South a chance to take a winning finesse. South should take the ♣A, intending to lead the deuce later.

Dlr: South   ♠ A K 9 3
Vul: N-S   ♥ A J 10
                    ♦ 7 6 4
                    ♣ Q 7 5

                    ♠ J 10
                    ♥ Q 6 4
                    ♦ K
                    ♣ A K J 8 6 4 2

WEST	NORTH	EAST	SOUTH
			1♣
Pass	1♠	Pass	3♣
Pass	6♣	All Pass	

Your partner's jump to slam was aggressive, and your jump-rebid of 3♣ perhaps more so. But we've all landed at worse contracts than 6♣.

West leads the ♦A and shifts to the ♥9. The heart finesse doesn't look appetizing; the alternative is to finesse in spades for 12 tricks.

How do you play the slam?

****

A competent West wouldn't shift to a heart from three or four low cards. For all he would know, your hand could be J2,K53,K,AKJ8642, and a heart shift would pickle East's queen and concede the slam without a fight.

Take the heart finesse.

        ♠ 8 6 5   ♠ Q 7 4 2
        ♥ K 9 8 2   ♥ 7 5 3
        ♦ A J 8 5 3   ♦ Q 10 9 2
        ♣ 9   ♣ 10 3

Dlr: South   ♠ K Q 5
Vul: N-S   ♥ K Q J 9 2
           ♦ A 4 3
           ♣ Q 9

           ♠ A
           ♥ 7 4
           ♦ K Q 5 2
           ♣ A K 7 6 4 3

WEST	NORTH	EAST	SOUTH
			1♣
Pass	2♥	Pass	3♦
Pass	3 NT	Pass	4♣
Pass	4♦	Pass	6♣
All Pass			

You reached the second-best slam; 6NT would have had more chances. Against 6♣ West leads the ♠J. You take the ace, cash the ♣A and lead to the ♣Q. Alas, East discards a spade. You pitch your hearts on the ♠KQ. Now you have options: A 3-3 diamond break will bring success, and so will a squeeze or a winning ruffing finesse in hearts.

What is your plan?

****

Lead the ♥K, intending to throw a diamond if East fails to cover. Though one of the alternative plays may work, East is marked with the ♥A. If West had it plus a sure trump trick, he would have tried to cash his ace.

     ♠ J 10 9   ♠ 8 7 6 4 3 2
     ♥ 10 5   ♥ A 8 6 3
     ♦ J 9 7 6   ♦ 10 8
     ♣ J 10 5 2   ♣ 8

Dlr: South
Vul: N-S

♠ K Q 2
♥ A Q 7 4
♦ 8 7 5
♣ Q 8 2

♠ 6 4 3
♥ K 5
♦ A K 3
♣ K J 10 5 4

WEST	NORTH	EAST	SOUTH
			1♣
Pass	1♥	Pass	1 NT
Pass	3 NT	All Pass	

West leads the ♠J. Some pairs have the agreement that the lead of the jack denies a higher honor. In their methods, the proper systemic lead from, say, K-J-10-7-3, would be the ten. But your current opponents have no such agreement.

How do you intend to make 3NT?

****

Your contract is at risk only if the defenders take four spades and the ♣A. You are safe if the spades are split 4-3. If you play a low spade from dummy at the first trick, you will go down if West had A-J-10-9-4 plus the ♣A for an entry. But with that holding, almost all Wests would have overcalled 1♠ at favorable vulnerability.

Play dummy's ♠2.

♠ J 10 9 8 5
♥ 8 2
♦ J 9 4
♣ A 6 3

♠ A 7
♥ J 10 9 6 3
♦ Q 10 6 2
♣ 9 7

You would go down if you played a spade honor from dummy.

Dlr: South   ♠ 8 5 3
Vul: N-S   ♥ A K 4 3
              ♦ Q J 5 3
              ♣ 8 7

              ♠ K 10 4
              ♥ 7 5
              ♦ A K 4 2
              ♣ A Q 4 3

WEST	NORTH	EAST	SOUTH
			1 NT
Pass	2♣	Pass	2♦
Pass	3 NT	All Pass	

West leads the ♠6, and East takes the ace and returns the nine. Suppose you take your king. A hold-up play has little to gain, and you may benefit from saving your last spade as a possible throw-in card. West follows with the deuce, suggesting that he led from a five-card suit.

When you run the diamonds, East follows twice, then discards the ♥J and ♣5. West lets go the ♣2.

How do you continue?

****

East's discard of the ♥J is revealing. It indicates a sequential holding but also suggests that East began with five hearts. Players often find it easy to make their first discard the "idle fifth" card in a suit. Cash the ♥AK, removing West's hearts, and lead dummy's last spade.

        ♠ Q J 7 6 2   ♠ A 9
        ♥ Q 6   ♥ J 10 9 8 2
        ♦ 10 8 7   ♦ 9 6
        ♣ K 9 2   ♣ J 10 6 5

After West takes three spades, he will have to lead a club to your A-Q.

East could afford to discard one club: On the bidding, you couldn't have the A-K-Q (and if you did, 3NT was unbeatable). East could discard one heart but not two since you might have held the ♥Q.

Dlr: South   ♠ 8 6 4 2
Vul: N-S   ♥ A 10 9 3
                    ♦ 4 2
                    ♣ 7 5 3

                    ♠ A Q 3
                    ♥ 6 4 2
                    ♦ A K 7 5
                    ♣ A K Q

WEST	NORTH	EAST	SOUTH
			2 NT
Pass	3♣	Pass	3♦
Pass	3 NT	All Pass	

West leads the ♠5: deuce, king, ace. You lead a heart, West puts up the king, and you duck to keep in touch with dummy. East plays the eight. Another spade goes to East's ten, and you play low.

East shifts to the ♦J, and you take the ace and lead a second heart. West plays the queen, dummy plays low again and East follows with the seven. You win West's ♠J return, as East throws a club. When you lead a third heart, West follows with the five.

Do you play the ace or finesse with the ten?

****

Play the ace. West would have led a heart from K-Q-J-5 instead of a spade from J-9-7-5.

♠ J 9 7 5	♠ K 10
♥ K Q 5	♥ J 8 7
♦ Q 9 3	♦ J 10 8 6
♣ J 4 2	♣ 10 9 8 6

Incidentally, South had my idea of a 2NT opening. Many modern players open 2NT with 19 points, though the logic of preempting your own auction by starting it at the three level escapes me.

Dlr: South
Vul: N-S

♠ K 6 2
♥ K J 9 2
♦ J 9 6 2
♣ K 6

♠ J
♥ A 5 3
♦ A K Q 10 5 3
♣ A J 4

WEST	NORTH	EAST	SOUTH
			1♦
Pass	1♥	Pass	3♣
Pass	4♦	Pass	4♥
Pass	5♣	Pass	6♦
All Pass			

You reach a good 6♦ after describing your hand with a improvised jump-shift followed by a show of heart support.

West leads the ♥8, which looks, walks and quacks like a singleton. You play dummy's nine, East's ten covers and your ace wins. You can see 11 tricks and can try for one more in spades. An endplay is also conceivable.

How do you play to make your slam?

****

Given that West led a singleton heart (a doubtful choice, to be sure, but a heart lead from a low doubleton or tripleton would have been even more questionable), East has the ♠A. If West had it, he would not try for a ruff, especially by leading a suit your side bid and supported; if East had an entry, the slam would fail anyway.

Draw trumps, take your high clubs, ruff your low club in dummy and run all the trumps. Dummy will be left with the ♠K and ♥KJ, and you will have the ♠J and two low hearts. You will have no trouble judging East's last three cards. If he saves the ♠A and ♥Q10, you will exit with a spade to endplay him.

♠ Q 9 8 5 4
♥ 8
♦ 8 4
♣ Q 10 7 5 2

♠ A 10 7 3
♥ Q 10 7 6 4
♦ 7
♣ 9 8 3

```
Dlr: South          ♠ 7 6 2
Vul: E-W            ♥ K Q 5 3
                    ♦ 8 3 2
                    ♣ K 6 5


                    ♠ A K 5 4
                    ♥ A 6 2
                    ♦ Q J 9 4
                    ♣ Q 10
```

WEST	NORTH	EAST	SOUTH
			1 NT
Pass	2♣	Pass	2♠
Pass	2 NT	All Pass	

Rejecting the belief that there is game in every deal, you bail out at 2NT. West leads the ♣4, and your ten wins when East follows with the eight. You lead a heart to dummy -- West plays the ten, East the nine -- and return the ♦2: five, jack, ace. West continues with the ♣A and a third club, dummy's king wins and East follows.

If the hearts break 3-3, you have eight tricks, but the defenders' carding suggests otherwise. Suppose you lead a second diamond from dummy. East plays the six.

Do you finesse with the nine or put up the queen?

****

The problem has elements of "restricted choice," but a strong inference is available. If West lacked a side entry to his long clubs, he would have led a second low club, not the ♣A and another, to keep a link with East. Finesse with the ♦9.

```
        ♠ J 9 3              ♠ Q 10 8
        ♥ 10 4               ♥ J 9 8 7
        ♦ A K 7              ♦ 10 6 5
        ♣ A J 7 4 3          ♣ 9 8 2
```

West can win and cash two clubs, but you will take the rest.

Perhaps you should have risked testing the hearts before you led that second diamond. West might have had J3,1074,AK10,AJ743.

```
Dlr: East          ♠ J 6
Vul: N-S           ♥ J 6 3
                   ♦ A Q J 3
                   ♣ A Q 10 4


                   ♠ Q 10 5
                   ♥ A 10 9 8
                   ♦ 5 2
                   ♣ K J 6 3
```

WEST	NORTH	EAST	SOUTH
		Pass	Pass
Pass	1♦	Pass	1♥
Pass	2♣	Pass	2 NT
Pass	3 NT	All Pass	

I don't care for North's bidding -- he suggested a two-suited hand when he doesn't have one -- but at least it let you become declarer at 3NT, which is always an advantage. Of course, you did your part by bidding 2NT at your second turn instead of raising North's 2♣ to 3♣.

West leads the ♠4: six, eight, ten. How will you win nine tricks and lose no more than four?

****

If the diamond finesse won, you would have three diamonds, four clubs, a spade and a heart. That would be the winning play if West held AKxxx,xx,Kxx,xxx, but with that hand he would have opened in third position or overcalled.

If you finesse in diamonds and find East with the king, you will be in trouble even if you lose only three spades; you will almost surely lose a fifth trick. Instead, plan to take two heart finesses, hoping for three hearts, four clubs, a diamond and a spade. This line of play is not dangerous. West would have overcalled with ♠AKxxx and a high heart and would have opened in third seat with AKxx,KQx,xxx,xxx.

```
       ♠ A K 7 4              ♠ 9 8 3 2
       ♥ K 7 2                ♥ Q 5 4
       ♦ 9 7 6                ♦ K 10 8 4
       ♣ 8 5 2                ♣ 9 7
```

Dlr: South
Vul: Both

♠ 3
♥ K 6
♦ K 9 6 3
♣ K Q 10 8 5 2

♠ A Q J 9 7 5 2
♥ A 4
♦ Q 8 4
♣ J

WEST	NORTH	EAST	SOUTH
			1♠
Pass	2♣	Pass	4♠
All Pass			

After your slap-dash auction to 4♠, West leads the ♥J. You win in your hand and lead the ♣J, and West takes the ace and leads a second heart to dummy. When you try to cash the ♣K, East ruffs low. You overruff and lead the ♠A and ♠Q, and West takes the king. East follows; all the trumps are in.

West next leads the ♦5: three, ten, queen. When you return a diamond toward dummy, West plays the seven.

Do you play the nine or the king?

****

Play the king. Give the defenders credit. If West started with J-7-5, he would have exited with a heart when he took the ♠K, forcing you to break the diamonds yourself and lose two more tricks.

♠ K 6	♠ 10 8 4
♥ J 10 8	♥ Q 9 7 5 3 2
♦ A 7 5	♦ J 10 2
♣ A 9 7 4 3	♣ 6

```
Dlr: South          ♠ 10 4
Vul: Both           ♥ K J 5
                    ♦ K 7 3 2
                    ♣ A J 9 3


                    ♠ A K Q J 9 8
                    ♥ A Q
                    ♦ Q 6
                    ♣ Q 10 6
```

WEST	NORTH	EAST	SOUTH
			1♠
Pass	2♣	Pass	3♠
Pass	3 NT	Pass	6♠
All Pass			

You roar into 6♠, giving West a minimum of help with his opening lead. He leads the ♥10, and when you see dummy, it seems you may have won your gamble. The slam is unbeatable if you can place the cards.

After you take the ♥A, how do you continue?

****

You can always make 6♠ if you guess which defender holds the ♦A. You will lead a low diamond through him. If he grabs the ace, you have two diamonds, six trumps, three hearts and a club. If he ducks, you win, discard your last diamond on dummy's hearts and finesse in clubs, possibly making an overtrick.

Who has the ♦A? If West, he might have led it after the bashing auction you had. Lead a trump to dummy and return the ♦2.

```
♠ 7 3                      ♠ 6 5 2
♥ 10 9 8 7 3               ♥ 6 4 2
♦ J 5 4                    ♦ A 10 9 8
♣ 7 4 2                    ♣ K 8 5
```

Even if you misplace the ♦A, you can still fall back on the club finesse.

Dlr: South   ♠ A Q 10 5 3
Vul: Both   ♥ J 5
                ♦ A K Q 6 2
                ♣ 8

                ♠ 8 4
                ♥ 9 6 4
                ♦ 3
                ♣ A K J 9 7 4 2

WEST	NORTH	EAST	SOUTH
			3♣
Pass	5♣	All Pass	

North's jump to 5♣ showed faith in the quality of your preempts -- and perhaps in your dummy play. Granted, even if 5♣ is down off the top, West might have to find a heart lead to beat it.

As it is, West leads the ♥K. He continues with the ♥2, and East takes the ace and shifts to the ♦10.

How do you manage the trump suit?

****

The percentage play in trumps is to finesse with the jack, but to adopt that play here would insult East. He knew from West's lead of the ♥2 that you started with three hearts. If East's clubs were Q-x-x, he would have led a third heart, forcing dummy to ruff and assuring a defensive trump trick.

Take the ♣AK.

♠ K 7 6	♠ J 9 2
♥ K Q 7 2	♥ A 10 8 3
♦ J 8 7 4	♦ 10 9 5
♣ Q 6	♣ 10 5 3

Dlr: North   ♠ A K J 4
Vul: Both   ♥ Q 7
                ♦ K 6
                ♣ J 6 5 4 2

                ♠ Q 10 9 7 6 2
                ♥ A 3
                ♦ 5 3
                ♣ A K 7

WEST	NORTH	EAST	SOUTH
	1♣	Pass	1♠
Pass	2♠	Pass	4♠

West leads the ♦Q, winning. He shifts to the ♥J.

Who has the ♥K? How do you play?

****

West wouldn't lead from the ♥K when he could easily lead a second diamond to East's ace to get a heart switch. Play low from dummy, preserving the ♥Q, and take your ♥A. Draw trumps and cash the ♣AK. If both defenders play low, exit with a red card, hoping East has no more clubs and must yield a ruff-sluff.

     ♠ 5   ♠ 8 3
     ♥ J 10 9 5   ♥ K 8 6 4 2
     ♦ Q J 10 4 2   ♦ A 9 8 7
     ♣ Q 10 8   ♣ 9 3

South goes down if he covers the ♥J with the queen.

Dlr: South   ♠ 4 3 2
Vul: E-W   ♥ 9 7 2
       ♦ 4 3 2
       ♣ A K 10 4

       ♠ A K Q 8 7
       ♥ K Q J
       ♦ 10 7 5
       ♣ 9 3

WEST	NORTH	EAST	SOUTH
			1♠
Pass	2♠	All Pass	

Against your dull-looking 2♠ contract, West leads the ♦9. East takes the jack, queen and king, then cashes the ♥A. West signals with the three, but East leads a second heart to your queen.

The contract seems to present no further problem, which means you must be careful. How do you continue?

****

East's defense is strange. Once West signalled no liking for hearts, East knew you had no more side-suit losers. His marked defense would be to lead the ♦A to promote a trump trick. Unlikely as it seems, East must hold the five missing trumps.

Go to the ♣A and return a trump. If East plays low, you will play the seven. When it holds, you take the A-K-Q and lead winners, losing only one trump trick.

  ♠   ♠ J 10 9 6 5
  ♥ 10 8 6 5 3   ♥ A 4
  ♦ 9 8 6   ♦ A K Q J
  ♣ Q 7 6 5 2   ♣ J 8

If East plays an intermediate on the first spade, win and go back to dummy for another spade lead. If East plays an intermediate again, you must duck. Then he will have to lead a trump, letting you pick up the trumps, or lead a diamond, letting you discard your last high heart and ruff with dummy's last trump. At the 11th trick, East's remaining ♠J65 will be trapped under your K-Q-8.

```
Dlr: North        ♠ Q 7 3
Vul: N-S          ♥ A J 10 3
                  ♦ 3 2
                  ♣ A K 5 2


                  ♠ K J 5
                  ♥ K Q 2
                  ♦ A J 8
                  ♣ 9 8 7 4
```

WEST	NORTH	EAST	SOUTH
	1♣	Pass	2 NT
Pass	3 NT	All Pass	

Against your 3NT, West leads the ♦5, and East plays the king.

To hold up your ace may be a winning play. So may be to win immediately. Which play do you choose?

****

To take nine tricks, you must force out the ♠A. If you think West has it, win the first diamond, keeping your J-8 as protection. If you think East has the ♠A, duck two diamonds and win the third in case West held Q-10-x-x-x.

Experienced declarers often rely on slender inferences; any inference is better than none. There is a slight indication that West has the ♠A: He led his own long suit instead of trying to find his partner's suit. If West held a hand such as 10642,74,Q10654,106, he might -- might -- have tried a major-suit lead.

I suggest winning the first diamond. If you preferred to duck twice, I hope you at least had a reason.

```
    ♠ A 10 9 2              ♠ 8 6 4
    ♥ 7 4                   ♥ 9 8 6 5
    ♦ Q 10 6 5 4            ♦ K 9 7
    ♣ 10 6                  ♣ Q J 3
```

```
Dlr: East              ♠ J 10 5
Vul: N-S               ♥ 7 5 2
                       ♦ A Q 10
                       ♣ K Q 6 2


                       ♠ A Q 8 6 4 2
                       ♥ A J 10
                       ♦ K 8
                       ♣ A 9
```

WEST	NORTH	EAST	SOUTH
		Pass	1♠
Pass	3♠	Pass	4♣
Pass	4♠	Pass	6♠
All Pass			

North's direct raise to 3♠ wouldn't have been my choice, and her failure to cuebid in response to South's 4♣ slam-try was mysterious. But this was the actual auction when the deal arose in a Women's Olympiad Teams.

West leads the ♥K, and you take the ace and set out to avoid losing a heart. You take three diamonds and then three clubs, and your ♥J10 go away; but West ruffs with the ♠9. She leads another diamond, and you ruff with the jack in dummy. When East discards a club, you underruff in your hand.

How do you play the trumps?

****

West has graciously arranged to put you back in dummy. If the trump finesse were going to work, she would have led the ♥Q, forcing you to ruff in your hand and lose the setting trick to the ♠K. Cash the ♠A.

```
   ♠ K 9                    ♠ 7 3
   ♥ K Q 8 4                ♥ 9 6 3
   ♦ J 7 6 3 2              ♦ 9 5 4
   ♣ J 4                    ♣ 10 8 7 5 3
```

Gail Greenberg drew the inference and dropped the ♠K. Cashing the ♠A early would have been a slight improvement.

Some players are reluctant to rely on inferences, or so they tell me, because they think their opponents can't be trusted to bid and play logically. That excuse won't fly in a world championship; but even if you're playing at your club, always assume that an opponent is operating correctly. If you do, and it turns out that he has done something silly, you won't feel guilty; you can laugh about it. But if you assume that your opponent has erred when he has played correctly, you will feel terrible.

CHAPTER 6

Getting information

Counting can enable declarer to place a missing card or suggest its location. Sometimes the count will fall into his lap; the bidding and early play may clear up the situation. But in many cases, declarer must go looking for information. To form a picture of the missing hands, he attacks the other suits, postponing the play of the crucial suit until the end.

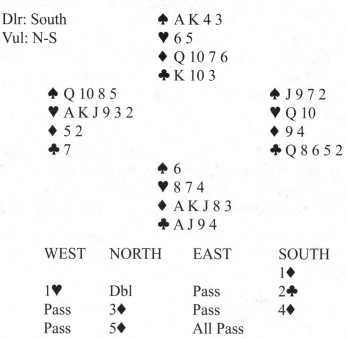

```
Dlr: South          ♠ A K 4 3
Vul: N-S            ♥ 6 5
                    ♦ Q 10 7 6
                    ♣ K 10 3
  ♠ Q 10 8 5                      ♠ J 9 7 2
  ♥ A K J 9 3 2                   ♥ Q 10
  ♦ 5 2                           ♦ 9 4
  ♣ 7                             ♣ Q 8 6 5 2
                    ♠ 6
                    ♥ 8 7 4
                    ♦ A K J 8 3
                    ♣ A J 9 4
```

WEST	NORTH	EAST	SOUTH
			1♦
1♥	Dbl	Pass	2♣
Pass	3♦	Pass	4♦
Pass	5♦	All Pass	

North's double was negative, showing four cards in spades. A 1♠ response would promise five.

West cashes two hearts and leads a third, hoping East can overruff dummy. Declarer ruffs with the ten, and East discards a club. East started with two hearts, West with six.

South draws trumps, finding a 2-2 break; he knows about eight of West's 13 cards. To get a complete count, South can play spades: He takes the A-K and ruffs a spade. When both defenders follow, declarer can go back to dummy with a high trump and ruff the last spade.

No matter what happens in spades, South will have his count. When the suit actually breaks 4-4, South's guess for the ♣Q becomes a sure thing. West had 4-6-2-1 pattern, so South can lead a club to the king and let the ten ride.

If West showed out on the third spade, marking him with 3-6-2-2 shape, South might still be apt to play East for the ♣Q, following the four-to-two odds.

```
Dlr: South          ♠ A 8 5
Vul: Both           ♥ 10 9 3 2
                    ♦ K J 5
                    ♣ K 7 5


                    ♠ K 6
                    ♥ K Q J 8 5
                    ♦ A 10 4 2
                    ♣ 6 3
```

WEST	NORTH	EAST	SOUTH
			1♥
Pass	3♥	Pass	4♥
All Pass			

The North hand doesn't fit my conception of a limit raise, but players have their own ideas. Against 4♥, West leads the ♣2. East wins with the jack and leads a trump, and West takes the ace and continues with the ♣Q. You ruff the third club and draw another trump, East-West following.

To make 4♥, you must locate the ♦Q. Suppose you wisely postpone your guess by taking the ♠KA and ruffing a spade. East follows three, four and seven; West follows deuce, nine, jack.

How do you play the diamonds?

****

West presumably had four clubs to lead the deuce, and he has no more spades. If he started with J-10-9-2 or Q-J-9-2, his opening lead would have been a spade from his sequence, not a club from a broken suit.

Give West 3-2-4-4 pattern. Other factors being equal, the odds are four to two that he has the ♦Q.

```
♠ J 9 2              ♠ Q 10 7 4 3
♥ A 7                ♥ 6 4
♦ Q 9 7 3            ♦ 8 6
♣ Q 10 4 2           ♣ A J 9 8
```

```
Dlr: South          ♠ K 5
Vul: Both           ♥ K Q 5
                    ♦ 7 6 5 4 2
                    ♣ A K 6


                    ♠ A Q J 10
                    ♥ A 10 3 2
                    ♦ A 9
                    ♣ Q 7 3
```

WEST	NORTH	EAST	SOUTH
			1 NT
Pass	4 NT	Pass	6 NT
All Pass			

The value of the North hand is diminished because the long suit contains no honors. North was worth a try for slam -- but just barely.

West leads the ♠9, and you win with the ten. All seems to depend on winning four heart tricks or on an unlikely squeeze.

What do you lead at the second trick?

****

A count may be helpful. To start looking for one, lead the ♦9, which also has the benefit of rectifying the count for a squeeze. Suppose East wins with the queen and leads another spade. You win and take two more spades, three clubs and the ♦A.

As it happens, West follows to four spades. He discards a diamond on the third club, and East discards a club on the ♦A. So West's pattern was 4-2-5-2.

```
♠ 9 8 7 6              ♠ 4 3 2
♥ 6 4                  ♥ J 9 8 7
♦ K J 10 8 3           ♦ Q
♣ 9 8                  ♣ J 10 5 4 2
```

Cash the ♥KQ and lead a third heart to finesse with the ten. If East had followed suit to the ♦A, you would have played to drop the ♥J. On a different lie of the East-West cards, a red-suit squeeze might be indicated.

```
Dlr: East                    ♠ Q 10 8
Vul: N-S                     ♥ Q 6 4
                             ♦ A 10 9 4
                             ♣ 9 7 2


                             ♠ A K J 9 6 4
                             ♥ K
                             ♦ K 6 3
                             ♣ A K 3
```

WEST	NORTH	EAST	SOUTH
		2♥	Dbl
Pass	2 NT	Pass	3♠
Pass	4♠	Pass	6♠
All Pass			

You had a reasonable auction to a decent slam. In many partnerships, North's 2NT response would have been conventional (asking you to bid 3♣), preparatory to showing a weak hand. That method can work well or badly.

Against 6♠ West leads the ♥9, and East takes the ace and returns a heart. You ruff and cash the ♠AK. Both defenders follow. You have 11 tricks and need to set up a third diamond for one more; how do you exercise your options?

****

East started with six hearts for his weak two-bid and two trumps. For more information, cash the ♣AK. East follows with the jack and then discards a heart.

How do you continue?

****

It appears that East's pattern was 2-6-4-1. Take the ♦KA next. As it happens, West plays the five and jack, so you discard your last diamond on the ♥Q and let the ♦10 ride for a ruffing finesse through East.

```
♠ 5 2                        ♠ 7 3
♥ 9 8 3                      ♥ A J 10 7 5 2
♦ J 5                        ♦ Q 8 7 2
♣ Q 10 8 6 5 4               ♣ J
```

If East had followed to two clubs, you would play him for 2-6-3-2 pattern, discarding a diamond on the ♥Q and ruffing a diamond. (If East had started with a low singleton diamond or with honor-x, the slam would be unmakable.)

Dlr: West   ♠ Q 10 9 3
Vul: N-S   ♥ 8 4
                 ♦ A Q 9
                 ♣ A 9 7 3

                 ♠ A K J 8 5
                 ♥ J 6 5
                 ♦ J 4 2
                 ♣ 6 4

WEST	NORTH	EAST	SOUTH
1♥	Dbl	Pass	2♠
3♥	3♠	Pass	4♠
All Pass			

You reach 4♠ after some serious overbidding. North had no business bidding 3♠, even in competition. You had nothing to spare for your invitational jump to 2♠; your ♥J was a wasted point.

West cashes the ♥KA and leads a third heart. You ruff with the ten in dummy, and East discards a diamond. West probably has the ♦K, but you still face a possible diamond loser.

How do you play?

****

Test the clubs. At the fourth trick, lead a low club from dummy. East puts up the king and shifts to a trump, and you win with the ace, take the ♣A and ruff a club high. Both defenders follow. When you lead a second trump to dummy's nine, West discards a heart. You ruff the last club, and West discards another heart.

What next?

****

You know West had one trump, six hearts and three clubs. Since he had three diamonds, a double finesse is correct. Lead the ♦J. When West covers, come back to your last trump and try a diamond to the nine.

     ♠ 4   ♠ 7 6 2
     ♥ A K Q 10 7 3   ♥ 9 2
     ♦ K 10 3   ♦ 8 7 6 5
     ♣ Q 10 2   ♣ K J 8 5

If West had followed to the fourth club, you would have led low to the ♦Q.

Dlr: West   ♠ J 3
Vul: Both   ♥ J 8 7 3 2
              ♦ Q 10 4 3
              ♣ 9 5

              ♠
              ♥ A K Q 10 9 6 4
              ♦ A 8 2
              ♣ A 7 2

WEST	NORTH	EAST	SOUTH
3♠	Pass	4♠	5♥
All Pass			

I know experts who would have shot out 6♥ with the South hand. If dummy had K-Q-x-x-x in either minor suit, that would be enough to offer a play for 13 tricks.

Against the cautious 5♥, West leads the ♠K, and you ruff high, lead a trump to dummy -- West throws a spade -- and ruff the last spade. You have a sure club loser, and the diamonds present a guess.

It can't hurt to delay by cashing the ♣A and conceding a club. West wins with the ten and leads the ♣K, and you ruff in dummy.

How do you continue?

****

Since West has shown one minor-suit king in addition to his good spades, East probably has the other minor-suit king. For West to open 3♠ wuth a hand such as KQ108764,--,K75,K106 would be atypical. Come back to your hand with a trump and lead a low diamond to dummy's ten.

♠ K Q 9 8 7 6 4	♠ A 10 5 2
♥	♥ 5
♦ 9 7 5	♦ K J 6
♣ K 10 6	♣ Q J 8 4 3

East takes the jack but is endplayed. He would have done better to bid 5♠, but the vulnerability was intimidating.

Dlr: West
Vul: None

♠ Q 3
♥ A K 5
♦ J 9 4 3 2
♣ 9 5 4

♠ A K J 10 8
♥ 6 4
♦ A 8 6 5
♣ Q 3

WEST	NORTH	EAST	SOUTH
3♣	Pass	Pass	3♠
Pass	4♠	All Pass	

This contract is pushy, but opposing preempts can make constructive bidding imprecise.

West starts with the ♣K and ♣A. East follows once, then discards a heart. When West continues with the ♣J, you ruff and draw trumps. You fear a 5-1 break, but trumps obligingly break 3-3.

How do you plan to attack the diamonds?

****

Although it may cost you an extra undertrick, take dummy's ♥AK to see what happens. Say West follows with the seven and jack. What next?

****

Now you know West had a singleton diamond, and to play him for the singleton ten is your only legitimate chance. Lead the ♦J from dummy.

♠ 9 5 2
♥ J 7
♦ 10
♣ A K J 10 7 6 2

♠ 7 6 4
♥ Q 10 9 8 3 2
♦ K Q 7
♣ 8

There is also the possibility of a defensive error. If East holds Q-10-7 or K-10-7, he may cover the ♦J.

If West had shown up with a singleton heart, you would expect a 2-2 diamond break.

```
Dlr: South          ♠ J 10 5 4 3
Vul: Both           ♥ A 7 5 2
                    ♦ 10 3
                    ♣ J 6


                    ♠ A K Q 7 6
                    ♥ Q 8 6 3
                    ♦ A K Q 7
                    ♣
```

WEST	NORTH	EAST	SOUTH
			1♠
Pass	2♠	3♣	4♣
Pass	4♥	Pass	6♠
All Pass			

Many experts would have chosen North's 4♥ cuebid since they could show the heart control without going beyond game. In my opinion, North wasn't compelled to cuebid when he had a high-card minimum for his raise to 2♠, including a wasted ♣J.

West leads the ♣3, and you ruff East's ten and draw trumps with the ace and jack. East had two trumps. You ruff dummy's last club and take your high diamonds, discarding a heart from dummy. Suppose both defenders follow, and when you lead your last diamond, West discards a club. You ruff in dummy and must go after the hearts.

How do you proceed?

****

East surely had at least six clubs to come in at the three level (and West's opening lead confirms this). East had two trumps and four diamonds, hence one heart at most. Lead a low heart from dummy and play low from your hand. The defender who wins will be endplayed; he must lead from the ♥K or concede a ruff-sluff.

```
♠ 8                      ♠ 9 2
♥ K J 10 4               ♥ 9
♦ 8 5 4                  ♦ J 9 6 2
♣ 9 7 5 3 2             ♣ A K Q 10 8 4
```

If East discarded on your third high diamond, you might play him for 2-3-2-6 pattern. You would lead to the ♥A and return a heart to your queen. If West won, he would be endplayed.

If West followed to the fourth diamond, suggesting that his pattern was 1-3-4-5, you would have a guess. If West held the ♥K, you could discard another heart from dummy for a loser-on-loser endplay. But since East bid at the three level, I suspect I would ruff the fourth diamond and play East for the ♥K.

```
Dlr: West              ♠ Q 7 5 3
Vul: Both              ♥ A J
                       ♦ 8 6 5 3
                       ♣ A Q 4


                       ♠ 4
                       ♥ K Q 10 9 6 4
                       ♦ K J
                       ♣ J 10 5 3
```

WEST	NORTH	EAST	SOUTH
1♠	Pass	Pass	2♥
Pass	2 NT	Pass	4♥
All Pass			

West leads the ♠K. East plays the deuce, and West shifts to a trump. West probably has the ♣K (and if he doesn't, he may have the ♦AQ and you will be sunk). Still, your fourth club is a concern.

Suppose you take the ♥A and lead to your ♦J. West probably has the ace, but East may have the queen. Alas, West wins with the queen and leads a second trump. You win in dummy and lead a second diamond to your king and West's ace. He leads a third diamond to East's nine, and you ruff.

You draw the last trump, learning that East had three, and lead a low club to the queen, winning. Next, you ruff dummy's last diamond. East discards a spade.

What play do you make in clubs?

****

All the evidence is gathered. West had five spades, two hearts and four diamonds, hence just two clubs. Lead a low club.

```
      ♠ A K 10 9 8           ♠ J 6 2
      ♥ 8 7                  ♥ 5 3 2
      ♦ A Q 10 2             ♦ 9 7 4
      ♣ K 2                  ♣ 9 8 7 6
```

Leading a club honor from your hand at any point would cost the contract.

Dlr: North
Vul: Both

♠ K 5 2
♥ 6 5 3
♦ A 10 6
♣ A Q 10 3

♠ A 8 3
♥ A 9 2
♦ K 5 3 2
♣ K 5 4

WEST	NORTH	EAST	SOUTH
	1 ♣	Pass	2 NT
Pass	3 NT	All Pass	

West leads the ♥7, and you duck East's jack and queen. West overtakes with the king and leads a third heart to your ace. East discards the ♠Q.

You have eight top tricks and good chances for nine. More than one approach is possible, but to start with a diamond to dummy's ten is reasonable. Suppose East wins with the jack and leads the ♠J.

To win, keeping a threat in spades, might gain. If East held QJ10xx,QJ,Jx,J9xx, you could succeed by strip-squeezing him. But say you duck the ♠J, and East leads another spade. West follows, and you take the king.

How do you continue?

****

Cash the ♦AK. If diamonds break 3-3, you have nine tricks. Suppose East turns up with four diamonds. Next you take the ♠A, and West throws a heart. You know West's pattern was 2-5-2-4, so you can continue with the ♣AK. If East follows low, lead a club to dummy's ten.

♠ 7 4
♥ K 10 8 7 4
♦ 8 4
♣ J 7 6 2

♠ Q J 10 9 6
♥ Q J
♦ Q J 9 7
♣ 9 8

If West had three spades, you would give him 3-5-2-3 pattern and play to drop the ♣J. East would not have discarded the ♠Q unless he had four or more.

100

Dlr: West   ♠ 5 4 3 2
Vul: Both   ♥ A Q 9 2
                 ♦ A J 5 2
                 ♣ 2

                 ♠
                 ♥ J 4 3
                 ♦ K Q 10 9 4 3
                 ♣ K Q 4 3

WEST	NORTH	EAST	SOUTH
1♣	Pass	1♠	2♦
2♠	6♦(!)	All Pass	

East-West play "support doubles," so West's raise to 2♠ promised four-card support; with three-card support he would have doubled. North made a "master bid" (a cynic's term for a doubtful bid) when he leaped to 6♦. He was willing to play you for either a spade void or the ♣A, and a heart finesse was a favorite to win if you needed it.

West leads the ♠K, and you ruff. If you go down at a makable slam, the fault will be yours, especially since you could have had a bit more for your 2♦ bid.

Endeavor to get a count in hearts. Lead the ♣Q to West's ace. He returns a spade, and you ruff, ruff a club in dummy, ruff another spade, ruff your last low club and draw trumps; West has a doubleton in trumps. Then cash your ♣K.

Suppose East shows out. How do you play the heart suit?

****

West had four spades, two diamonds and five clubs, hence two hearts. Lead a low heart to dummy's queen and cash the ace.

♠ K Q 8 6	♠ A J 10 9 7
♥ K 5	♥ 10 8 7 6
♦ 8 6	♦ 7
♣ A 10 8 6 5	♣ J 9 7

If East followed to the ♣K, you would play West for 4-3-2-4 pattern and lead the ♥J, planning a later finesse with the nine.

"Support doubles" are popular but lose in many situations. In this deal, it was nice of the opponents to tell you how the spades were divided. It might have been awkward for you to find out in the play.

Dlr: West   ♠ A 5
Vul: N-S   ♥ A 7 3
                    ♦ A 4 3 2
                    ♣ Q 10 9 7

                    ♠ K J
                    ♥ K 6 4
                    ♦ K Q 9 5
                    ♣ A J 6 4

WEST	NORTH	EAST	SOUTH
3♠	Pass	Pass	3 NT
Pass	6 NT	All Pass	

Nobody knows precisely what your 3NT as South shows. You could have had a weaker hand with a long suit, a medium hand such as Kx,Kx,KQJxxx,Axx or a balanced hand with 21 HCP. North's leap to slam was speculative, but so would have been any other action.

West leads the ♠10. You win in dummy and let the ♣10 ride, winning. The ♣9 also holds, West following low. Now four tricks in diamonds will see you home.

How do you continue?

****

Play a low heart from both hands. If West wins and leads another spade to your king, and East follows, cash the ♥AK and ♣A. Assuming West had a seven-card spade suit for his preempt, you will have a count. West's pattern might have been 7-3-1-2 or 7-4-0-2.

     ♠ Q 10 9 8 6 4 3   ♠ 7 2
     ♥ J 9 2   ♥ Q 10 8 5
     ♦ 6   ♦ J 10 8 7
     ♣ 8 3   ♣ K 5 2

Take the ♦A and lead a second diamond, playing the nine if East follows low. If instead he splits his honors, win and go back to the ♣Q for another diamond lead.

Dlr: East   ♠ A Q J
Vul: None   ♥ K J 7 6
              ♦ 10 7 3
              ♣ A 6 5

              ♠ K 3
              ♥ A Q 10 9 4 2
              ♦ A 9 4 2
              ♣ 10

WEST	NORTH	EAST	SOUTH
		4♣	4♥
Pass	6♥	All Pass	

You let East's preempt tempt you into an unsound 4♥ overcall. (If opportunity came disguised as temptation, just one knock would be enough.) North had his 6♥ bid.

West leads the ♣3, and you take the ace. How do you proceed?

****

At trick two, ruff a club high. West throws a spade, so East had eight clubs. You draw trumps (West had two) and cash your spade winners. East follows twice and discards a club.

Now what do you do in diamonds?

****

East's pattern was 2-1-2-8. Ruff dummy's last club, go back to dummy with a trump, lead a diamond to your ace and exit with a diamond. The slam is cold if both of East's diamonds are honors; he will be endplayed. If East started with K-x, he will have to play second hand high to avoid an endplay. If East has Q-x. West will have to rise with the king (a "crocodile coup") to save his partner.

     ♠ 9 8 6 5 4 2   ♠ 10 7
     ♥ 8 5   ♥ 3
     ♦ K 8 6 5   ♦ Q J
     ♣ 3   ♣ K Q J 9 8 7 4 2

If East followed to three spades, marking him with one diamond at most, you could lead a low diamond without cashing the ace. You could expect to succeed by endplaying East since West might have led the ♦K from K-Q-J-x-x.

Even better, you could cash the ♦A, lead a trump to dummy and return the last club, discarding a diamond. East would be endplayed.

```
Dlr: South          ♠ A K 10
Vul: Both           ♥ Q J
                    ♦ A 6 3 2
                    ♣ J 9 6 2


                    ♠ Q J 5
                    ♥ A K 10
                    ♦ Q J 5
                    ♣ A Q 5 3
```

WEST	NORTH	EAST	SOUTH
			1♣
Pass	1♦	Pass	2 NT
Pass	6 NT	All Pass	

West leads the ♦10, and East takes the king and returns a diamond to your queen. You cash the ♦J, and East throws a heart. Next you lead a heart to dummy and return a club: four, queen, eight.

You must diagnose the club position. West's eight suggests that he might have had the doubleton 10-8, but an expert West would unhesitatingly falsecard with 10-8-7.

Before you commit yourself, take your heart and spade winners and the ♦A. Suppose West follows to three spades but discards on the third heart.

How do you continue?

****

You know East held three spades, six hearts and two diamonds, so two clubs. Lead a low club from dummy.

```
♠ 8 7 4 3              ♠ 9 6 2
♥ 5 4                  ♥ 9 8 7 6 3 2
♦ 10 9 8 7            ♦ K 4
♣ 10 8 7              ♣ K 4
```

If instead your count showed East with three clubs, you would lead the jack, hoping to pin West's ten.

Dlr: East ♠ 7 4
Vul: Both ♥ J 9 7 4
♦ A Q 7 5
♣ A 9 8

♠ K J 8 5
♥ A K Q 10 5
♦ 4
♣ 7 5 4

WEST	NORTH	EAST	SOUTH
		Pass	1♥
Pass	3♥	Pass	4♥
All Pass			

West leads the ♦2. Plan the play.

****

You could take the ♦A and hope for good luck in spades, but it seems unlikely that East has both the ace and queen. He didn't open the bidding, may have the ♦K and certainly has at least one club honor.

So the contract may boil down to a spade guess, which you would like to postpone. A finesse with the ♦Q at the first trick may win and will break even if it loses since you can discard a club on the ♦A.

Suppose East takes the ♦K and shifts to the ♣K. You duck, and he continues with the ♣J. You take the ace, pitch your last club on the ♦A and lead a spade.

When East plays low, do you play the king or the jack?

****

Play the jack. You have found that East, who didn't open, has the ♦K and presumably the ♣KQJ. He won't have the ♠A but may have the ♠Q.

♠ A 10 9 3 ♠ Q 6 2
♥ 8 3 ♥ 6 2
♦ J 8 6 2 ♦ K 10 9 3
♣ 10 6 2 ♣ K Q J 3

```
Dlr: South          ♠ 8 6 2
Vul: N-S            ♥ K 4
                    ♦ A K 3
                    ♣ K Q 10 6 3


                    ♠ A K Q 4
                    ♥ A Q 7
                    ♦ Q 7 5
                    ♣ A 9 4
```

WEST	NORTH	EAST	SOUTH
			2 NT
Pass	4♣	Pass	4 NT
Pass	7 NT	All Pass	

North used Gerber to check for aces. When you showed three, he shot the moon.

West leads the ♥J. The grand slam looks like a heavy favorite. Say you take the ♥K and cash the top spades. If spades break 3-3, you have 13 tricks; but East follows with the nine and jack and throws a diamond on the third spade. Next you cash the ♥AQ. East throws another diamond; he had two hearts.

How do you continue?

****

You know West had four spades and six hearts. Take the ♦Q and ♦K. If West discards, clubs are 3-2. If instead he follows suit, cash the ♣K and lead a club to your nine. You can take the ♣A and return to dummy with the ♦A to cash the ♣Q.

```
♠ 10 7 5 3              ♠ J 9
♥ J 10 9 6 5 2          ♥ 8 3
♦ 6 4                   ♦ J 10 9 8 2
♣ 2                     ♣ J 8 7 5
```

It was lucky the card gods dealt you the ♣9.

CHAPTER 7

Discovery and anti-discovery

An attempt to locate a missing high card in one suit by attacking another is a "discovery" play.

The process of counting the hands, treated in other chapters, is a discovery play in a sense, but the term is generally applied in a situation where high-card points are at issue.

```
Dlr: West          ♠ J 10 4
Vul: Both          ♥ K 8 7 3
                   ♦ 9 5 2
                   ♣ Q 10 3
      ♠ A K 7                        ♠ 9 6 2
      ♥ 6 5 2                        ♥ Q 4
      ♦ 8 7 6 3                      ♦ A K 10
      ♣ A 8 5                        ♣ 9 7 6 4 2
                   ♠ Q 8 5 3
                   ♥ A J 10 9
                   ♦ Q J 4
                   ♣ K J
```

WEST	NORTH	EAST	SOUTH
Pass	Pass	Pass	1♥
Pass	2♥	All Pass	

West leads the ♠K. When East signals with the deuce, West shifts to a diamond, and East takes the K-A and leads a third diamond.

Declarer must locate the ♥Q, and the defender who holds the ♣A can't have it; then he would have had enough points to open the bidding, So declarer solves his problem in trumps by leading the ♣K to discover who has the ace.

Dlr: West   ♠ K 9 7 5
Vul: Both   ♥ Q 4
                   ♦ A 8 7 2
                   ♣ 7 5 2

                   ♠ A Q 10 6 2
                   ♥ 10 5
                   ♦ Q
                   ♣ A Q 8 6 3

WEST	NORTH	EAST	SOUTH
1♥	Pass	2♥	2♠
Pass	3♠	Pass	4♠
All Pass			

West cashes the ♥K and ♥A. He gets out with a trump, and you draw trumps in two rounds. A club finesse with the queen figures to lose; nevertheless, West could have enough points to open without the ♣K.

How do you resolve the problem?

****

East needs one good card for his raise to 2♥, so the minor-suit kings should be split. At the fifth trick, lead the ♦Q, expecting West to cover if he has the king. If he covers, you will play East for the ♣K; but if West plays low, you will take the ♦A and attack the clubs by leading the ♣A and a low club.

     ♠ 8 4   ♠ J 3
     ♥ A K J 7 3   ♥ 9 8 6 2
     ♦ J 9 5 4   ♦ K 10 6 3
     ♣ K 4   ♣ J 10 9

```
Dlr: North          ♠ A 9 8 7
Vul: Both           ♥ Q 9 3
                    ♦ A 5 4
                    ♣ K J 4


                    ♠ Q 10
                    ♥ A K J 10 8 7
                    ♦ Q 6 2
                    ♣ A Q
```

WEST	NORTH	EAST	SOUTH
	1♣	Pass	2♥
Pass	3♥	Pass	4♣
Pass	4♦	Pass	4♥
Pass	4♠	Pass	6♥
All Pass			

North-South do well to stop at 6♥. If I had been South, I would have worried that North had longer clubs. A hand such as A98,Q93,A4,KJ432 would make 7NT almost cold. But perhaps North would have bid a grand slam if he held that hand.

Against the small slam, West leads the ♣10 to your ace. You have 11 tricks. You can go after a second spade trick, or you can discard a spade on dummy's third high club and try for a second diamond trick. (But West's opening lead and East's failure to double North's 4♦ cuebid suggest that West has the ♦K.)

How do you play?

****

You could go to dummy and lead the ♠7. Many an East would put up the king if he had it, but a capable East might duck, leaving you with a nasty guess.

A discovery play is available. Lead the ♠Q. If West has both the king and jack, he will surely cover; to play low would be superhuman. Then you can take the ace, draw trumps, concede a spade and claim.

If West plays low on the ♠Q, you can place East with one missing spade honor. Take the ace, cash the ♥A and ♥J, take two more clubs to discard your ♠10, and lead the ♠7 from dummy. You will take two ruffing finesses through East, at least one of which will work, to set up your 12th trick with a middle spade.

```
♠ 6 5 2              ♠ K J 4 3
♥ 5 4                ♥ 6 2
♦ K 9 8 7            ♦ J 10 3
♣ 10 9 8 7           ♣ 6 5 3 2
```

```
Dlr: West          ♠ K 9 7 2
Vul: N-S           ♥ 10 9 5 3
                   ♦ Q
                   ♣ A Q 8 2


                   ♠
                   ♥ A Q J 8 6 4
                   ♦ A K 6 2
                   ♣ 7 4 3
```

WEST	NORTH	EAST	SOUTH
Pass	Pass	Pass	1♥
Pass	3♣	Pass	6♥
All Pass			

North's 3♣ response -- a jump-shift by a passed hand -- promised a good heart fit and club values. North would jump only because your opening bid improved his hand, not because he passed a hand some players would have opened. (An alternative would have been a "splinter" jump to 4♦.)

West leads the ♦9 to dummy's queen. You can discard two clubs from dummy on the ♦AK, so you will make the slam if you avoid a loser in trumps or clubs.

Can a discovery play help you place the cards?

****

East probably has the ♠A -- if West had it, he might have led it -- but you may find out for sure by leading the ♠K at the second trick. If East covers -- surely he would -- you ruff and next try the club finesse.

If it wins, fine; if not, you know East, who didn't open in third position at favorable vulnerability, had the ♠A, ♣K, ♦J and probably a second spade honor since West might have led the ♠Q from Q-J-x-x. The ♥K would give East a 12-point hand, and most Easts would have opened. You would play to drop the singleton ♥K with West.

```
♠ Q 10 8 6 5 3          ♠ A J 4
♥ K                     ♥ 7 2
♦ 9 8 7                 ♦ J 10 5 4 3
♣ J 9 6                 ♣ K 10 5
```

110

```
Dlr: South        ♠ 6 5
Vul: N-S          ♥ K 5 4 2
                  ♦ 9 7 5 2
                  ♣ K J 3


                  ♠ A K
                  ♥ A Q 3
                  ♦ A 8 6 4 3
                  ♣ Q 10 4
```

WEST	NORTH	EAST	SOUTH
			1♦
Pass	1♥	Pass	2 NT
Pass	3 NT	All Pass	

West leads the ♠J to your king. You have six top tricks and, given time, plenty of possibilities for at least three more. But if the defenders get in twice, they will establish and then cash enough spade tricks to beat 3NT.

How do you play?

****

The temptation is to go after your longest suit: If diamonds break 2-2, you will have four diamonds, two spades and at least three hearts. But if the diamonds break 3-1, you must instead force out the ♣A and hope for a 3-3 heart break, giving you four hearts, a diamond, two clubs and two spades.

Therefore, test the hearts. If the suit breaks 3-3, you force out the ♣A. If hearts don't break evenly, take the ♦A, lead a second diamond and hope for the best.

```
♠ J 10 9 4 2        ♠ Q 8 7 3
♥ 10 8 6            ♥ J 9 7
♦ Q                 ♦ K J 10
♣ A 9 7 2          ♣ 8 6 5
```

Dlr: North   ♠ 9 5 3
Vul: N-S   ♥ A Q 4
                     ♦ A Q J 9
                     ♣ A 7 3

                                  ♠ K J 4
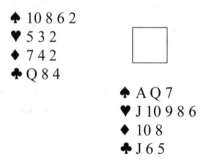   ♥ K 7
                                  ♦ K 6 5 3
                                  ♣ K 10 9 2

WEST	NORTH	EAST	SOUTH
	1 NT	Pass	2♣
Pass	2♦	Pass	2♥
Pass	4♥	All Pass	

South's bidding suggests eight or so points with a five-card heart suit and invites game.

Against 4♥, West leads the ♠2, and dummy plays low.

Plan your defense.

****

Defensive discovery plays are uncommon -- defenders are seldom in control of the play and have neither the time nor the opportunity -- but such plays do come along. Here, East should be careful to play the jack on the first spade. He knows declarer has the ♠A and can discover who has the queen.

♠ 10 8 6 2
♥ 5 3 2
♦ 7 4 2
♣ Q 8 4

                      ♠ A Q 7
                      ♥ J 10 9 8 6
                      ♦ 10 8
                      ♣ J 6 5

South's ♠Q wins, and he loses a trump finesse next. East can count 10 potential winners for declarer: two spades, four trumps, three diamonds and a club. The defense needs four winners first. Perhaps a spade return will set up one spade trick, but a spade, a trump and a diamond won't be enough.

East must try for two clubs, a diamond and a trump. He should shift to the ♣10.

If South had won the first spade with the ace, East would know to try for two spades, plus a trump and a diamond.

```
Dlr: South          ♠ 7 5
Vul: N-S            ♥ K Q 5
                    ♦ K 9 6 3
                    ♣ K Q 8 4
     ♠ A 6 4 2
     ♥ J 10 6 4
     ♦ 4                ┌─────┐
     ♣ J 10 9 5         │     │
                        └─────┘
```

WEST	NORTH	EAST	SOUTH
			1♠
Pass	2 NT	Pass	3♦
Pass	3 NT	Pass	4 NT
Pass	5♣	Pass	5♠
All Pass			

North's 2NT response was, by agreement, natural and forcing. North-South stop at 5♠ after South's inquiry for aces elicits a disappointing reply.

You lead your singleton diamond: three, eight, ace. Declarer leads the ♠K. How do you defend?

****

South's Blackwood 4NT bid said that he was concerned only about missing aces; your partner has an ace, but North-South should have no other losers.

If you grab your ♠A, you must guess how to put East in to give you a ruff. Play low on declarer's first and second trump leads. By the time he leads a third trump, your partner will be able to offer a helpful signal.

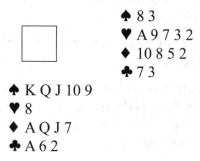

```
                          ♠ 8 3
      ┌─────┐             ♥ A 9 7 3 2
      │     │             ♦ 10 8 5 2
      └─────┘             ♣ 7 3
            ♠ K Q J 10 9
            ♥ 8
            ♦ A Q J 7
            ♣ A 6 2
```

After East flags the ♥9 on the third spade, you will know what to do. Really, you should have doubled 5♠ inferentially, but only if you were going to defend correctly.

North-South need to upgrade their bidding system so they can stop at a safer level.

```
Dlr: North          ♠ K 9 3
Vul: E-W            ♥ A Q 4
                    ♦ A 3 2
                    ♣ K 9 8 5


                    ♠ A J 8 7 4
                    ♥ K J 10 3
                    ♦ 8 4
                    ♣ 6 2
```

WEST	NORTH	EAST	SOUTH
	1 NT	Pass	2♣
Pass	2♦	Pass	3♠
Pass	4♠	All Pass	

West leads the ♥9. You play low from dummy and win with the ten, as East signals with the deuce. You have a diamond and at least one club to lose, plus a problem in trumps. It appears you need a favorable lie in one of the black suits.

How do you approach the play?

****

A safety play is available to lose no more than one trump trick. You can cash the ♠A, lead the four and play dummy's nine if the defenders contribute low cards. If East can win, you draw the last trump with the king later. If West discards on the second trump, take the king and return a third trump toward your jack.

But you don't know whether you can afford the luxury of the safety play. If East has the ♣A, you must bring in the trump suit for no losers.

At trick two, lead a club to the king. If it wins, play safe in trumps. If East has the ♣A, start the trumps by leading low from dummy, intending to finesse with the jack. You will cater to the singleton queen with East (and pay off to a falsecard from the doubleton Q-10).

```
♠ Q 10 5 2              ♠ 6
♥ 9 8 6                 ♥ 7 5 2
♦ Q 9 5                 ♦ K J 10 7 6
♣ A J 4                 ♣ Q 10 7 3
```

Dlr: West
Vul: N-S

♠ J 4 3 2
♥ A
♦ K 8 4 2
♣ A K J 3

♠ K
♥ J 6 4
♦ Q 7 6 5 3
♣ Q 10 6 4

WEST	NORTH	EAST	SOUTH
Pass	1♣	Pass	1♦
Pass	1♠	Pass	2♣
Pass	3♦	Pass	5♦
All Pass			

West leads the ♥K. You have a spade and a trump to lose. All depends on avoiding a second trump loser. How do you play?

****

You want to lead the first trump through the defender who holds the ace in case it is singleton. At the second trick, lead the ♠J from dummy for a fake finesse. You might induce East to duck with the ace. If West produces the ♠A, you will know East has the ♦A since West has shown the ♥KQ and passed as dealer.

If East climbs up with the ♠A, you might still be inclined to play him for the ♦A. If West had five hearts (not certain but possible) to the K-Q plus the ♦A, he might have tossed in a passed-hand overcall.

♠ A 8 7 6
♥ K Q 7 3
♦ J 10 9
♣ 8 2

♠ Q 10 9 5
♥ 10 9 8 5 2
♦ A
♣ 9 7 5

Dlr: North ♠ J 3
Vul: Both ♥ 10 7 6
  ♦ A K Q J
  ♣ K Q 9 6

♠ A 7 4
♥ K 8 3 2
♦ 8 5
♣ A J 5 2

WEST	NORTH	EAST	SOUTH
	1♦	Pass	1♠
Pass	2♣	Pass	2♠
Pass	3♠	Pass	4♠
All Pass			

Many Norths would have opened 1NT despite the lack of a stopper in both majors. After North chose a different way to describe his hand, he might have passed 2♠.

You lead the ♥2: six, jack, ace. Declarer leads a trump to the jack and a trump back to his king. East follows with the five and deuce, indicating that he had three trumps.

After you take your ace, what do you lead?

****

You can see two more defensive tricks: the ♣A and a heart. On the play to the first trick, South is marked with the ♥9, so at least one heart will cash. The fourth trick must be a second heart or a club ruff.

Presumably, declarer has three or more diamonds. If he had only two, he would have tried to discard a losing heart on the diamonds before he led trumps. Did he have KQ1098,A9,743.1074 or KQ1098,A94,743,107?

To discover, shift to the ♣J, marooning declarer in dummy. East will signal count; he will know, on the bidding, that you have the ♣A. If he signals high, you will give him a club ruff later; if he signals low, you will try to cash a second heart.

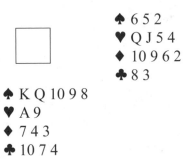

♠ 6 5 2
♥ Q J 5 4
♦ 10 9 6 2
♣ 8 3

♠ K Q 10 9 8
♥ A 9
♦ 7 4 3
♣ 10 7 4

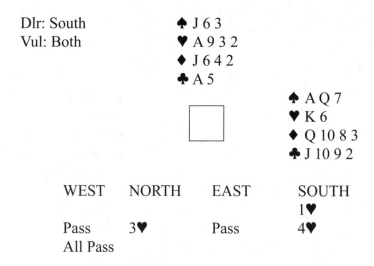

Dlr: South   ♠ J 6 3
Vul: Both   ♥ A 9 3 2
                   ♦ J 6 4 2
                   ♣ A 5

                             ♠ A Q 7
                             ♥ K 6
                             ♦ Q 10 8 3
                             ♣ J 10 9 2

WEST	NORTH	EAST	SOUTH
			1♥
Pass	3♥	Pass	4♥
All Pass			

West leads the ♠2, and dummy plays the three. Plan your defense.

****

Put on the queen as a discovery play. If declarer has K-9-x, he can take the king; but you will defend passively for the rest of the deal. If declarer has four losers, he will still lose them.

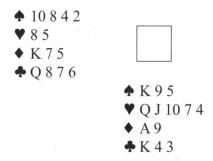

♠ 10 8 4 2
♥ 8 5
♦ K 7 5
♣ Q 8 7 6

                 ♠ K 9 5
                 ♥ Q J 10 7 4
                 ♦ A 9
                 ♣ K 4 3

After South takes the ♠K, he can succeed, but only with double-dummy play.

On this layout, it would be costly to take the ♠A and continue. It might also be costly to play the ace and shift: West might have the ♠K after all, and South might hold K-Q-x in clubs.

Against a suit contract, East might make a similar play in this position:

K43

2 led >>   Q105

South is marked with the ace. If dummy plays low, East can play the ten to learn who has the jack.

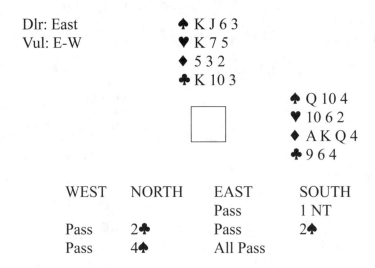

Dlr: East
Vul: E-W

♠ K J 6 3
♥ K 7 5
♦ 5 3 2
♣ K 10 3

♠ Q 10 4
♥ 10 6 2
♦ A K Q 4
♣ 9 6 4

WEST	NORTH	EAST	SOUTH
		Pass	1 NT
Pass	2♣	Pass	2♠
Pass	4♠	All Pass	

West pleases you by leading the ♦10. Plan your defense. (Look ahead.)

****

Suppose you win the first diamond with the queen, as per normal procedure, and cash the king. South's jack falls, and he ruffs your ♦A next. He takes the ♠A, loses a finesse with dummy's jack to your queen and wins the trump return.

South then claims, announcing that he will play your partner for the ♣Q. The South and West hands are

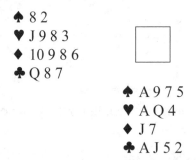

♠ 8 2
♥ J 9 8 3
♦ 10 9 8 6
♣ Q 8 7

♠ A 9 7 5
♥ A Q 4
♦ J 7
♣ A J 5 2

South had a guess for the ♣Q, but after he found you with the top diamonds and the ♠Q, he recalled that you were a passed hand. Then he knew who had the ♣Q.

"Concealment" is a subtle defensive skill that takes experience and foresight, but a good defender must be alert to refute declarer's efforts to place the cards. If you win the first diamond with the ace, cash the queen and lead your low diamond, declarer will have a chance to go wrong.

Dlr: North ♠ Q J 8 5
Vul: N-S   ♥ A K 9 3 2
            ♦ J 10
            ♣ 9 2

                          ♠ 10 3
                          ♥ Q 10 8 7
                          ♦ A 6 3
                          ♣ K J 8 3

WEST	NORTH	EAST	SOUTH
	Pass	Pass	1♠
Pass	3♥	Pass	3♠
Pass	4♠	All Pass	

North's passed-hand jump-shift showed spade support. South's 3♠ signed off; North bid game anyway.

West leads the ♥J, won by the ace. Declarer takes the A-Q of trumps, West following, and next leads the ♣2 from dummy.

Plan your defense.

****

Put up the ♣K. This can lose nothing: If South has the ace and queen, he is about to win the finesse anyway. But if he lacks the ♣A and has a guess in diamonds, you can feed him some misinformation.

If your ♣K wins, lead a low diamond.

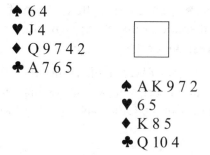

♠ 6 4
♥ J 4
♦ Q 9 7 4 2
♣ A 7 6 5

                          ♠ A K 9 7 2
                          ♥ 6 5
                          ♦ K 8 5
                          ♣ Q 10 4

South knows from the opening lead that you have the ♥Q and knows you lacked the values to open the bidding. If he thinks you have the ♣AK, he will go wrong in diamonds.

An active effort by a defender to prevent a discovery play is known as "anti-discovery." If you play low on the first club, South will put on his ten, losing to West's ace. Then there is some danger that West will err by shifting to a diamond; and even if West exits safely, South may wind up guessing the diamond position.

South could have tried to set up dummy's hearts for diamond discards. Perhaps he feared the opening lead was a singleton.

Dlr: South   ♠ Q
Vul: N-S   ♥ A Q
     ♦ A 10 8 6 5 2
     ♣ A 10 4 3

     ♠ A K J 3
     ♥ K J 10 6
     ♦ Q J 9 7
     ♣ 9

WEST	NORTH	EAST	SOUTH
			1♦
4♣	6♦	All Pass	

West leads the ♣K, and your fears are confirmed when East ruffs dummy's ace. He shifts to a spade. You can still make North's bid look good if you pick up the trump suit.

How do you play?

****

Delay your guess in trumps. Take the ♠A and lead the ♠K. If West ruffs, overruff in dummy and claim. If he follows suit, discard a heart from dummy and continue with the ♠J. If West ruffs that, overruff and claim. If instead he follows to the third spade or discards, throw dummy's last heart and lead your ♥K, putting West under the gun again.

Eventually, you will get a count of West's distribution. If for instance he follows to two spades and one heart, you will know his pattern was 2-1-2-8, and you can finesse in trumps. Otherwise, you will know to play to drop the king in East.

   ♠ 9 7   ♠ 10 8 6 5 4 2
   ♥ 8   ♥ 9 7 5 4 3 2
   ♦ K 3   ♦ 4
   ♣ K Q J 8 7 6 5 2 ♣

Dlr: East   ♠ A J 5 2
Vul: E-W   ♥ K 8 4 3
                      ♦ 10 3
                      ♣ A Q 6

                      ♠ K 10 8 4 3
                      ♥ Q
                      ♦ A 8 4
                      ♣ 7 5 4 2

WEST	NORTH	EAST	SOUTH
		Pass	Pass
Pass	1♣	Pass	1♠
Pass	2♠	Pass	3♠
Pass	4♠	All Pass	

For you, South, to pass North's raise to 2♠ would have been understandable, but you tried again and reached a pushy game.

West leads the ♦Q to your ace. A club to dummy's queen wins, so you're still alive. How do you continue?

****

Lead a heart to your queen. If West wins, you can place the ♠Q with East. West would have opened in third seat with the ♠Q, ♥A, ♦QJ and ♣K (plus, the ♥J and ♣J are out there somewhere).

Suppose East rises with the ♥A and returns a diamond, and West takes the jack and leads the ♣K. You take the ace, pitch a club on the ♥K, ruff a heart and ruff a diamond. By observing the fall of the cards, you may get some idea of which defender is more likely to have length in trumps.

         ♠ 6   ♠ Q 9 7
         ♥ A 9 5 2   ♥ J 10 7 6
         ♦ Q J 9 5   ♦ K 7 6 2
         ♣ K 10 8 3   ♣ J 9

Some Wests would have entered the auction with that hand. Personally, I wouldn't have acted even at a different vulnerability. The risk of helping declarer place the cards outweighs the chance of gaining anything.

Dlr: South   ♠ Q 10 8 3
Vul: None   ♥ 7 4
                  ♦ K 10 4
                  ♣ A K Q 2

                  ♠ A K J 9 5 2
                  ♥ K J 9 6 3
                  ♦
                  ♣ J 7

WEST	NORTH	EAST	SOUTH
			1♠
Pass	2 NT	Pass	4♥
Pass	5♣	Pass	6♠
All Pass			

North's 2NT was a conventional forcing spade raise. Your 4♥ showed heart length; a 3♥ bid would have shown heart shortness.

West leads a trump, and you draw trumps with the A-Q. You need a winning guess in hearts, if one exists, to make the slam. How do you continue?

****

Lead the ♦K from dummy. If East plays low, you will ruff and place the ♥A with East. If West had both red aces, surely he would have tried to cash the ♦A on opening lead, lest you discard a diamond loser on a high club in dummy.

If East covers the ♦K, you will ruff and place the ♥A with West, playing for split aces. There is also some chance that East would have doubled the slam with two aces.

      ♠ 7 4   ♠ 6
      ♥ Q 8 5   ♥ A 10 2
      ♦ A 9 7 5 2   ♦ Q J 8 6 3
      ♣ 10 6 4   ♣ 9 8 5 3

If East has only the ♦A and plays low smoothly when dummy leads the ♦K, he deserves to beat you.

CHAPTER 8

Counting on defense

Most players, from experts to novices, are convinced that defense is harder than declarer play. I think it's harder in the sense that defenders often face out-and-out guesses -- notably on opening lead. Nevertheless, many defensive problems admit to analysis. I believe it takes more time and effort to become a fine declarer because dummy play has so many aspects: psychological as well as technical.

Whatever your opinion, you will agree that counting is essential to consistently good defense. The defenders must try to reconstruct declarer's shape and high-card values. They must count his possible winners, which can resolve the basic problem of whether to defend actively or passively. They must count their own possible tricks to establish a goal and make necessary assumptions.

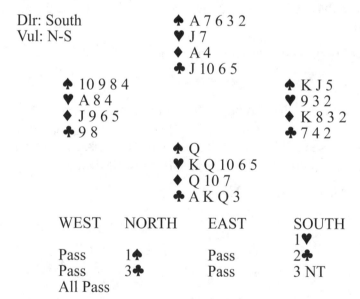

```
Dlr: South          ♠ A 7 6 3 2
Vul: N-S            ♥ J 7
                    ♦ A 4
                    ♣ J 10 6 5

  ♠ 10 9 8 4                      ♠ K J 5
  ♥ A 8 4                         ♥ 9 3 2
  ♦ J 9 6 5                       ♦ K 8 3 2
  ♣ 9 8                           ♣ 7 4 2

                    ♠ Q
                    ♥ K Q 10 6 5
                    ♦ Q 10 7
                    ♣ A K Q 3
```

WEST	NORTH	EAST	SOUTH
			1♥
Pass	1♠	Pass	2♣
Pass	3♣	Pass	3 NT
All Pass			

West leads the ♦5. If South could see all four hands, he would take the ♦A and start the hearts. But he plays low from dummy, and East's king wins.

East can assume from the auction that South had five hearts and four clubs. (If South had six hearts, he would have rebid the suit; with 5-5 in hearts and clubs, he would have been reluctant to play at notrump.) West's opening lead suggests four cards in diamonds, so South's pattern should be 1-5-3-4.

South surely had a diamond stopper to bid 3NT, and a diamond return may not beat 3NT even if he doesn't. East must shift to the ♠K in case South's singleton is the queen. If West has a trick in hearts or clubs -- and the defenders' cause is hopeless if he doesn't -- East-West will get that trick plus a diamond and three spades.

```
Dlr: South              ♠ Q 10
Vul: N-S                ♥ A J 2
                        ♦ K J 6 5 2
                        ♣ 7 6 3
        ♠ K 3
        ♥ 7 6 3
        ♦ A 7 3
        ♣ K 10 8 4 2
```

WEST	NORTH	EAST	SOUTH
			1♠
Pass	2♦	Pass	2♠
Pass	2 NT	Pass	3♥
Pass	4♠	All Pass	

You lead the ♣4, and East plays the queen. Declarer takes the ace and leads the ♦10.

You must play quickly. Do you win or duck?

****

To count declarer's shape, you must be familiar with basic bidding. South's sequence showed six spades, four hearts and minimum values. If he had extras, his second bid would have been 2♥ or 3♣. Since East's play of the ♣Q marks South with the ♣J, the ♦10 must be a singleton.

Grab your ♦A and cash the ♣K.

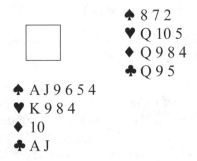

```
                              ♠ 8 7 2
                              ♥ Q 10 5
                              ♦ Q 9 8 4
                              ♣ Q 9 5
        ♠ A J 9 6 5 4
        ♥ K 9 8 4
        ♦ 10
        ♣ A J
```

After South ruffs the third club, he will lose finesses in both major suits to go down one. (If South happened to refuse the trump finesse and instead led the ♠A and another spade, you would need to shift to a heart to break up a potential red-suit squeeze on East.)

Dlr: West   ♠ Q 8 6 2
Vul: None   ♥ J 3
                   ♦ Q J 10 5 4
                   ♣ K 6

♠ K 4
♥ A Q 4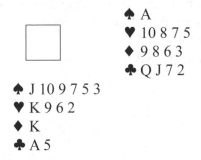
♦ A 7 2
♣ 10 9 8 4 3

WEST	NORTH	EAST	SOUTH
1♣	Pass	1♥	1♠
2♥	2♠	3♣	3♠
All Pass			

You lead the ♣10, and South wins in his hand with the ace and leads the ♦K: ace, four, nine.

What do you lead to trick three?

****

Count your tricks. To beat 3♠, you need five of them. You have a diamond in the bag but will get no more diamonds and no clubs. You need two tricks each in hearts and trumps.

To lead a low trump looks rash, but you have no choice but to hope East has the ♠A.

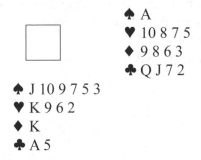

After East wins the third trick, a heart return will settle the matter. But if you mistakenly exit with a club to dummy's king at the third trick, South can make his contract.

125

Dlr: South   ♠ Q 9
Vul: Both   ♥ A Q J 8 4
         ♦ 9 4
         ♣ Q 10 6 5

♠ K J 7 2
♥ 7 5
♦ J 10 7 6 3
♣ K 4

WEST	NORTH	EAST	SOUTH
			1♣
Pass	1♥	Pass	1♠
Pass	3♣	Pass	3 NT
All Pass			

North's 3♣ jump-preference was invitational to game, not forcing. That treatment looks unsound since if South had to pass, North-South might miss a 5-3 heart fit. But it's not up to me and you to question North-South's bidding agreements.

You lead the ♦6: four, king, ace. Declarer leads a low heart to dummy's queen, winning, and lets the ♣10 ride to your king.

How do you continue?

****

Declarer surely has the ♥K. If East had it, his correct defense would have been to pounce on the second trick in order to return a diamond, setting up your suit while you still had an entry. The same idea would apply if East had the ♣A: He should grab the first club to return a diamond. So South's clubs are probably headed by the A-J, and he is also marked with the ♦AQ.

If South has the ♠A, the contract is unbeatable. Lead the ♠K.

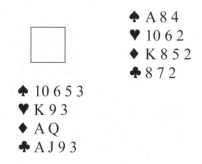

           ♠ A 8 4
           ♥ 10 6 2
           ♦ K 8 5 2
           ♣ 8 7 2

♠ 10 6 5 3
♥ K 9 3
♦ A Q
♣ A J 9 3

East will unblock his eight and win the next spade with the ace. Then a third spade will come through South's 10-6 to your J-7, giving the defense five tricks.

Dlr: South   ♠ K Q 7
Vul: Both   ♥ K 10 8 3
                ◆ K 9 8 2
                ♣ 6 3

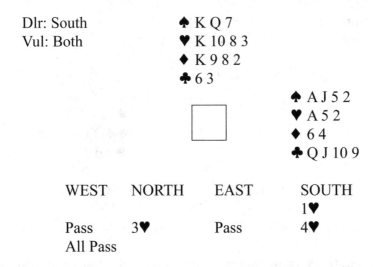

                        ♠ A J 5 2
                        ♥ A 5 2
                        ◆ 6 4
                        ♣ Q J 10 9

WEST	NORTH	EAST	SOUTH
			1♥
Pass	3♥	Pass	4♥
All Pass			

West leads the ◆Q. South wins with the ace and leads a trump: four, ten, ace.

How do you plan to beat the contract?

****

A shift to the ♣Q won't beat it. You have 12 HCP, and dummy has 11. If West has the ◆QJ, South needs the ♣AK to have his 4♥ bid. You must hope for a trump, a diamond and two spades. But even if declarer has a diamond loser, he can set up a third diamond trick with dummy's intermediates, hence you need your spade tricks in a hurry. Shift to the ♠2.

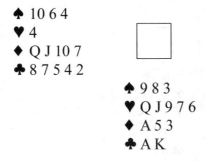

♠ 10 6 4
♥ 4
◆ Q J 10 7
♣ 8 7 5 4 2

                ♠ 9 8 3
                ♥ Q J 9 7 6
                ◆ A 5 3
                ♣ A K

East should assume a South hand that will let the defense prevail. If declarer had a third club and one fewer spade or diamond, the contract would be untouchable.

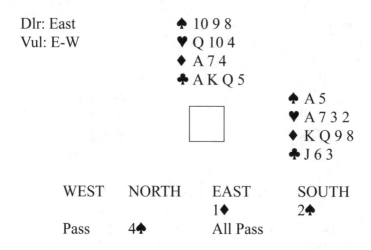

Dlr: East
Vul: E-W

♠ 10 9 8
♥ Q 10 4
♦ A 7 4
♣ A K Q 5

♠ A 5
♥ A 7 3 2
♦ K Q 9 8
♣ J 6 3

WEST	NORTH	EAST	SOUTH
		1♦	2♠
Pass	4♠	All Pass	

South's jump to 2♠ is preemptive; he will typically have a six-card suit and a weak hand.

West leads the ♦2. South takes dummy's ace and cashes the ♣AK, discarding a diamond. Next, he leads the ♠10 from dummy.

How do you defend?

****

If South had started with three diamonds, he would have pitched both losers on the high clubs. It appears that his pattern was 6-4-2-1. You best chance is to give West a third-round heart ruff. Rise with the ♠A and lead the ♥2.

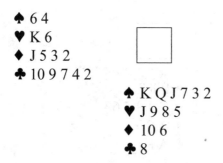

♠ 6 4
♥ K 6
♦ J 5 3 2
♣ 10 9 7 4 2

♠ K Q J 7 3 2
♥ J 9 8 5
♦ 10 6
♣ 8

Could the suggested defense lose -- if South held QJ7432,K985,106,8 -- by saving him a guess for the ♥J? I suppose so. But declarer might guess the ♥J anyway by counting your points and inferring from your failure to open 1NT. Anyway, it's better to rely on a legitimate defensive chance than on less-than-perfect dummy play.

West could have saved you trouble by leading the ♥K.

Dlr: North
Vul: N-S

♠ J 7
♥ J 10 9 5 3
♦ A
♣ A K J 9 6

♠ A Q 6
♥ A Q 2
♦ K 8 7 5 3
♣ 7 2

WEST	NORTH	EAST	SOUTH
	1♥	Pass	1♠
Pass	2♣	Pass	2 NT
Pass	3 NT	All Pass	

After managing to keep silent with your 15 HCP, you lead the ♦5 against 3NT. Dummy's bare ace wins, and East signals with the deuce. Declarer next leads the ♥3: eight, king, ace.

How do you continue?

****

South's 2NT bid suggests about 11 points, so East has none. Since South is marked with the ♣Q, he will have plenty of tricks after he sets up the hearts.

You can't expect to beat the contract with diamond tricks. South has at most five spades, did not support the clubs and appears (from East's signal) to have one heart. His diamonds are probably Q-J-x-x, and even if you lead another low diamond at the third trick and find East with the 10-9-2, he will never get in to lead a third diamond through South's remaining honor.

Your best and perhaps only chance is to play East for the ♠10. Cash the ♠A and lead the ♠Q.

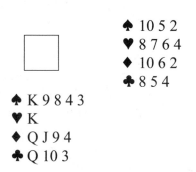

```
                              ♠ 10 5 2
                              ♥ 8 7 6 4
                              ♦ 10 6 2
                              ♣ 8 5 4
        ♠ K 9 8 4 3
        ♥ K
        ♦ Q J 9 4
        ♣ Q 10 3
```

Dlr: North
Vul: N-S

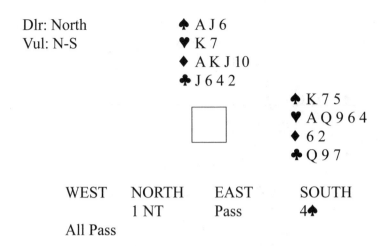

♠ A J 6
♥ K 7
♦ A K J 10
♣ J 6 4 2

♠ K 7 5
♥ A Q 9 6 4
♦ 6 2
♣ Q 9 7

WEST	NORTH	EAST	SOUTH
	1 NT	Pass	4♠
All Pass			

West leads the ♥3, and dummy plays low. You take your queen, but declarer ruffs your ♥A and leads the ♠Q, passing it to your king when West follows low.

What do you lead at trick four?

****

With dummy's diamonds slated to produce four tricks, it's tempting to shift to a club. But a count of South's tricks will guide you. South has no hearts, five spades and four diamonds; hence he can't make 4♠ without a club trick, and you need not lead the suit.

Return a trump and let declarer break the clubs.

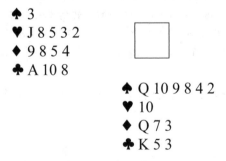

♠ 3
♥ J 8 5 3 2
♦ 9 8 5 4
♣ A 10 8

♠ Q 10 9 8 4 2
♥ 10
♦ Q 7 3
♣ K 5 3

If you lead a club, you give declarer a chance to make an impossible contract by guessing right. True, he should assume you haven't made a mistake; he should put up his ♣K and go down anyway. But if he played low instead, you would feel insulted as well as distressed at letting the contract make.

```
Dlr: North          ♠ J 3
Vul: N-S            ♥ A Q J 3
                   ♦ A K 6
                   ♣ 10 8 6 3
     ♠ A Q 2
     ♥ 7 5              ┌─────┐
     ♦ J 9 5 3 2        │     │
     ♣ A 5 2            └─────┘
```

WEST	NORTH	EAST	SOUTH
	1♣	Pass	1♠
Pass	1 NT	Pass	3♠
Pass	4♠	All Pass	

You lead the ♥7. Declarer wins with the king and leads the ace and queen, pitching the ♣K. You score your ♠2. What do you lead at the fourth trick?

****

Declarer had two hearts and presumably one club. For him to play that way with the doubleton ♣K would be bizarre and might cost a cold contract. If declarer had a seven-card trump suit, you won't beat 4♠, but assuming his distribution was 6-2-4-1, you must shift to a diamond.

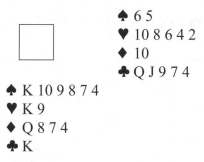

```
              ┌─────┐      ♠ 6 5
              │     │      ♥ 10 8 6 4 2
              └─────┘      ♦ 10
                          ♣ Q J 9 7 4
        ♠ K 10 9 8 7 4
        ♥ K 9
        ♦ Q 8 7 4
        ♣ K
```

When you win a high trump, you can give East a diamond ruff and score your other high trump for down one. Trying to cash the ♣A lets the contract make.

131

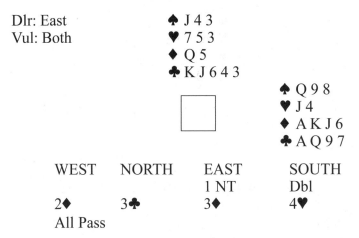

Dlr: East
Vul: Both

♠ J 4 3
♥ 7 5 3
♦ Q 5
♣ K J 6 4 3

♠ Q 9 8
♥ J 4
♦ A K J 6
♣ A Q 9 7

WEST	NORTH	EAST	SOUTH
		1 NT	Dbl
2♦	3♣	3♦	4♥
All Pass			

West's runout to 2♦ was natural. Against 4♥ he leads the ♦4. You win with the jack and try to cash the ace, but South ruffs. He takes the ♥AK, and West follows with the eight and then discards a diamond. Declarer next leads the ♣10: deuce, three ... and you take the queen.

What do you lead next?

****

This is an uneasy situation; you seem to be endplayed. Count. South had seven hearts and one diamond. If his pattern is 3-7-1-2, he can't make 4♥ without the ♠AK (unless you lead the ♣A now) and will always make it if he has both high spades. But West's ♣2 signal suggests that South's shape was 4-7-1-1.

You must assume that West has a high spade, but if South has A-10-x-x or K-10-x-x, a spade shift will cost the setting trick. Nor can you afford to lead the ♣A since South might ruff and get two spade discards on the ♣KJ.

Your correct lead is the ♣9.

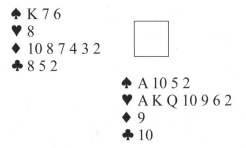

♠ K 7 6
♥ 8
♦ 10 8 7 4 3 2
♣ 8 5 2

♠ A 10 5 2
♥ A K Q 10 9 6 2
♦ 9
♣ 10

Declarer can discard a spade and take dummy's ♣J, but he will gain nothing since his fourth spade would be a winner anyway. He must break the spades and lose two more tricks.

If South's spades had been K-10-5-2, you could survive by leading a third diamond since South would not gain enough from the ruff-sluff to make the contract.

```
Dlr: South          ♠ 10 8 7 4
Vul: Both           ♥ J 5
                    ♦ J 9
                    ♣ Q J 10 9 3
    ♠ K 5
    ♥ A 7 6 2
    ♦ K Q 10 7
    ♣ K 5 4
```

WEST	NORTH	EAST	SOUTH
			1♠
Dbl	3♠	Pass	4♠
All Pass			

Over your double, North's competitive jump to 3♠ was weak and preemptive. With a stronger hand, he would have had options: a redouble or a conventional bid such as a 2NT response.

You lead the ♦K, and South takes the ace, cashes the ♠A and leads the ♠Q to your king as East follows. When you try to cash the ♦Q, South ruffs. He leads a trump to dummy and returns the ♣Q: six from East, seven, king.

What do you return?

****

East might have the ♥K, and with dummy's clubs a threat to provide discards, you may feel like trying for two heart tricks. Before you do anything, count. South had five spades and one diamond, so seven cards in hearts and clubs. After he runs dummy's clubs, he will still have two hearts.

Hence, you need not lead hearts, and to do so might cost. Exit with a club and wait for South to lead a heart himself.

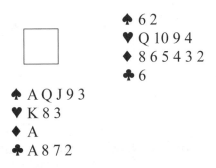

```
                         ♠ 6 2
                         ♥ Q 10 9 4
                         ♦ 8 6 5 4 3 2
                         ♣ 6
              ♠ A Q J 9 3
              ♥ K 8 3
              ♦ A
              ♣ A 8 7 2
```

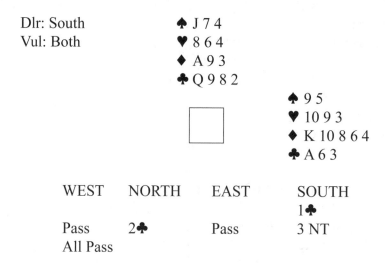

```
Dlr: South          ♠ J 7 4
Vul: Both           ♥ 8 6 4
                    ♦ A 9 3
                    ♣ Q 9 8 2
                                    ♠ 9 5
                                    ♥ 10 9 3
                                    ♦ K 10 8 6 4
                                    ♣ A 6 3
```

WEST	NORTH	EAST	SOUTH
			1♣
Pass	2♣	Pass	3 NT
All Pass			

West leads the ♥2, and declarer captures your nine with the queen. He leads the ♣K, West follows with the five and you duck. On the next club, West discards the ♠2, and you take your ace.

How do you defend?

****

To return partner's lead seems mandatory, but even if a heart return will net you three more tricks, you still need a fifth trick from somewhere. And if declarer has a second heart stopper, you must make something happen in spades or diamonds.

An inference is available from the opening lead. West had four hearts, from his lead of the deuce, and one club. If he had five spades, he would have led a spade. So the evidence indicates that West's pattern was 4-4-4-1: South shot out 3NT with a singleton diamond.

Shift to the ♦K.

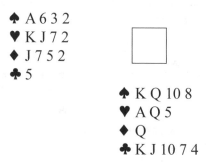

```
♠ A 6 3 2
♥ K J 7 2
♦ J 7 5 2
♣ 5
                    ♠ K Q 10 8
                    ♥ A Q 5
                    ♦ Q
                    ♣ K J 10 7 4
```

If you return a heart, the defense gets only four tricks.

134

Dlr: East   ♠ A 5
Vul: Both   ♥ 8 6 5
               ♦ K J 6 2
               ♣ A 10 9 4

                              ♠ K 9 3
                              ♥ A K 10 7 3
                              ♦ 8 7
                              ♣ K J 5

WEST	NORTH	EAST	SOUTH
		1♥	2♦
Pass	2♥	Pass	2♠
Pass	4♦	Pass	5♦
All Pass			

West leads the ♥2, and declarer's jack falls under your king. South ruffs the next heart and takes the ♦A and ♦K. West discards a heart. Declarer then ruffs dummy's last heart and leads the ♣Q: eight, four, king.

You seem to be caught in a spider's web; any return may cost. Can you escape the trap?

****

Count, count, count. South has six diamond tricks and no hearts. A club return will give him three tricks there -- nine in all -- and dummy's ♠A will make ten, but you will still score your ♠K.

A spade return would lose if South had the queen and, as is indicated, 4-1-6-2 pattern. A heart return would yield a ruff-sluff: Declarer could ruff in his hand, pitch dummy's low spade, take the ♣A and lead the ten to ruff out your jack. Dummy would be high, making five.

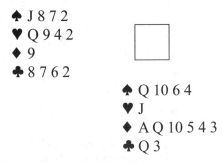

   ♠ J 8 7 2
   ♥ Q 9 4 2
   ♦ 9
   ♣ 8 7 6 2
                ♠ Q 10 6 4
                ♥ J
                ♦ A Q 10 5 4 3
                ♣ Q 3

Dlr: South
Vul: Both

```
                        ♠ K 5 3
                        ♥ 10 6
                        ♦ K J 10 4
                        ♣ K 10 6 2
    ♠ Q 10 7 2
    ♥ K J 8 5 3         ┌──────┐
    ♦ A 8 5 3           │      │
    ♣                   └──────┘
```

WEST	NORTH	EAST	SOUTH
			1♣
Dbl	1♦	1♥	1♠
2♥	3♣	Pass	4♣
Pass	5♣	All Pass	

After a lively auction, you lead the ♥5 against South's game. East comes through with the ace and returns the deuce. Declarer follows with the nine and queen, and your king wins.

What do you lead at the third trick?

****

Any lead looks perilous. If declarer has a diamond loser, he can't avoid it, and if you try to cash the ♦A and declarer ruffs it, he can get two diamonds winners in dummy for spade discards. A spade shift might find him with the ace and jack. A third heart lead might concede a fatal ruff-sluff.

To solve the problem, count declarer's tricks. He has at most seven clubs and two spades. (He followed to two hearts and bid spades, so he can't have an eight-card club suit.) You can afford to concede one diamond trick but not two. Then your ♠Q will score. Lead the ♦3.

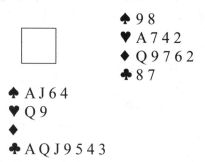

```
                        ♠ 9 8
   ┌──────┐             ♥ A 7 4 2
   │      │             ♦ Q 9 7 6 2
   └──────┘             ♣ 8 7
    ♠ A J 6 4
    ♥ Q 9
    ♦
    ♣ A Q J 9 5 4 3
```

South can put up dummy's king, pitching a spade, and assault you with seven rounds of trumps, but your last three cards will be the ♠Q107. No squeeze will operate since East will cling to his ♦Q. The 13th trick will belong to the defense.

Dlr: North   ♠ A 9 5 2
Vul: N-S   ♥ A 8 3
Matchpoints   ♦ A 10 7 2
                    ♣ J 5

♠ Q 4
♥ J 9 6 4
♦ J 6 3
♣ Q 10 7 2

WEST	NORTH	EAST	SOUTH
	1♦	Pass	1♠
Pass	2♠	Pass	4♠
All Pass			

You lead the ♣2 to the five, king and ace. Declarer leads a trump to the ace and back to his king, and East's jack and your queen fall together. Next, declarer takes the ♥KA, ruffs dummy's last heart and exits with the ♣9 to your queen.

You won't beat this contract, but overtricks matter. How do you defend?

****

Declarer had five spades and two hearts. If he has no more clubs, you can afford to lead another club. You will give up a ruff-sluff, but since declarer will have four diamonds, he won't gain anything; his fourth diamond would have been a winner anyhow. What you must avoid is breaking the diamond suit.

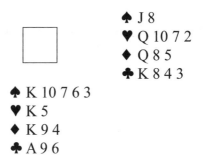

```
                    ♠ J 8
                    ♥ Q 10 7 2
                    ♦ Q 8 5
                    ♣ K 8 4 3
♠ K 10 7 6 3
♥ K 5
♦ K 9 4
♣ A 9 6
```

A club exit holds South to 11 tricks. A diamond exit lets him take 12 if he diagnoses the position.

In a practiced partnership, East could help West by following with the ♣3 -- signalling count -- on the second club lead.

```
Dlr: East            ♠ A K 8 3
Vul: N-S             ♥ 9 7 3
                     ♦ K J 7 6
                     ♣ J 5
   ♠ J 10 6
   ♥ Q 10 8 2        ┌─────┐
   ♦ Q 9 8           │     │
   ♣ A 7 2           └─────┘
```

WEST	NORTH	EAST	SOUTH
		Pass	Pass
Pass	1♠	Pass	1 NT
All Pass			

Defending low-level partscore contracts is taxing -- and 1NT is often the toughest -- because declarer's hand won't be well defined.

You lead the ♥2. Dummy is unexpected; North planned to pass any suit response, but his odd choice of opening bids risked missing a fit in a red suit. East puts up the ♥A and returns the ♥4. Declarer takes the king, and leads a diamond: eight, jack, ace. East produces a third heart, and you take the ten and queen. Dummy discards a spade, and declarer lets go two low diamonds.

When you shift to the ♠J, dummy wins, and East signals with the nine. Next, dummy leads the ♣J. East follows with the three, and South pauses for an instant and plays the king.

How do you defend?

****

Count points -- your partner's. He passed as dealer and has shown the ♥AJ and ♦A and clearly has the ♠Q, so he can't have the ♣Q.

Let the ♣K win. If you take your ace, declarer will cackle as he wins your spade return and runs the clubs for an overtrick.

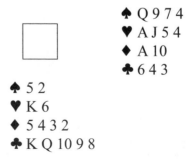

```
              ♠ Q 9 7 4
┌─────┐       ♥ A J 5 4
│     │       ♦ A 10
└─────┘       ♣ 6 4 3
   ♠ 5 2
   ♥ K 6
   ♦ 5 4 3 2
   ♣ K Q 10 9 8
```

After you duck the ♣A, the best declarer can do is take the ♦K and concede a diamond to escape for down one.

CHAPTER 9

How to see declarer's hand

No, I'm not recommending that you defend using a periscope to see declarer's hand, or strategically place a large mirror behind him, or sit atop a pile of cushions to get a clear view.

Because a defender operates under the handicap of seeing only dummy, he must try to reconstruct declarer's hand -- and his partner's hand as well -- through counting and drawing inferences from the bidding and play. He must see declarer's hand with his mind's eye.

Some inferences are stronger than others, often depending on declarer's degree of skill. You should always assume, however, that your partner is defending logically.

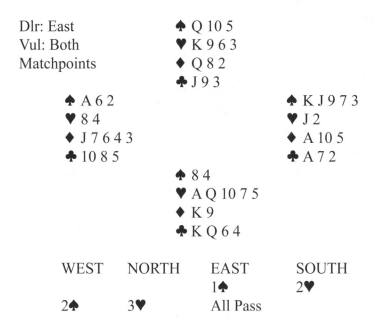

```
Dlr: East          ♠ Q 10 5
Vul: Both          ♥ K 9 6 3
Matchpoints        ♦ Q 8 2
                   ♣ J 9 3
        ♠ A 6 2                    ♠ K J 9 7 3
        ♥ 8 4                      ♥ J 2
        ♦ J 7 6 4 3                ♦ A 10 5
        ♣ 10 8 5                   ♣ A 7 2
                   ♠ 8 4
                   ♥ A Q 10 7 5
                   ♦ K 9
                   ♣ K Q 6 4
```

WEST	NORTH	EAST	SOUTH
		1♠	2♥
2♠	3♥	All Pass	

West led the ♦4, and when dummy played low, East put up the ace. Nervous about leading from the ♠K, East returned a low club. That let declarer make an overtrick by discarding a spade on the ♦Q, and East-West got a matchpoint zero.

East was critical of his partner's opening lead, but East should have inferred that West had the ♠A because he hadn't led the suit East-West had bid and raised. If West had only low spades, why would he have speculated by leading a diamond from four or five to the jack or king?

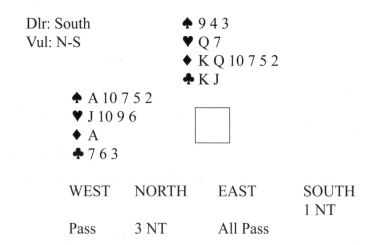

Dlr: South   ♠ 9 4 3
Vul: N-S   ♥ Q 7
                ♦ K Q 10 7 5 2
                ♣ K J

♠ A 10 7 5 2
♥ J 10 9 6
♦ A
♣ 7 6 3

WEST	NORTH	EAST	SOUTH
			1 NT
Pass	3 NT	All Pass	

South's 1NT opening bid promised 16 to 18 HCP. You lead the ♠5, East plays the jack and declarer wins with the queen. He leads a low diamond, and your ace wins. East follows with the three.

What do you do next?

****

Lead the ♠A. You can't hope to put in East for a spade return. You have nine HCP, dummy has 11. If declarer has 16, there aren't enough left for East to have an ace besides his ♠J.

You must hope declarer held only two spades, and that is quite possible; if he had K-Q-x, he would have won the first spade with the king. He won with the queen so you would know he had the king also.

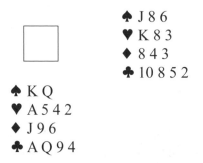

                        ♠ J 8 6
                        ♥ K 8 3
                        ♦ 8 4 3
                        ♣ 10 8 5 2
♠ K Q
♥ A 5 4 2
♦ J 9 6
♣ A Q 9 4

North-South would have done better at 5♦, but North's raise to 3NT was the correct percentage move. The nine-trick game would make more often.

West's problem would be harder at matchpoints since South could hold KQ6,A542,J96,AQ9. Then snatching the ♠A would concede a second overtrick.

Dlr: North   ♠ A Q 4
Vul: N-S   ♥ J 3
                ♦ Q J 4
                ♣ K Q 7 5 2

♠ K 10 3
♥ 10 8 5 4
♦ A 10
♣ A 9 6 3

WEST	NORTH	EAST	SOUTH
	1 NT	Pass	3♦
Pass	4♦	Pass	5♦
All Pass			

After East-West's natural auction to 5♦, you lead a heart. East covers dummy's jack with the king, and declarer takes the ace and leads a trump. How do you defend?

****

The defense will win no tricks in hearts or spades. Declarer can win a spade finesse and discard spades on dummy's clubs. The contract will fail if East has the ♦K, but that is impossible after he showed the ♥K. South's bidding suggests at least 10 HCP.

Your only chance for a third trick is to give East a club ruff. Rise with your ♦A and lead the ♣A and a second club.

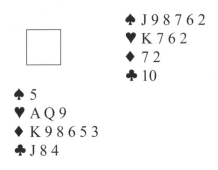

                  ♠ J 9 8 7 6 2
                  ♥ K 7 6 2
                  ♦ 7 2
                  ♣ 10

      ♠ 5
      ♥ A Q 9
      ♦ K 9 8 6 5 3
      ♣ J 8 4

Dlr: North
Vul: None

North hand:
♠ 8 7 6 5
♥ Q 10 4
♦ K Q
♣ K Q 3 2

West hand:
♠ A K 10 2
♥ 6 5 3
♦ A 4 3
♣ J 10 8

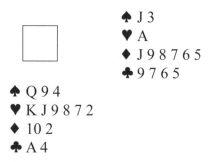

WEST	NORTH	EAST	SOUTH
	1♣	Pass	1♥
Pass	1 NT	Pass	3♥
All Pass			

South's jump-rebid is invitational to game, not forcing. You lead the ♠K, and East plays the jack, declarer the four.

How do you defend?

****

You can give East a third-round spade ruff, but a shift to an ace in his hand and a spade return will serve as well; and indeed, it seems he must have an ace for the defense to take five tricks.

Lead a trump. There is no rush to lead a club; if East has the ♣A, he will take it in time to return a spade, giving the defense three spades, a diamond and a club. But if South has the ♣A, he might benefit by discarding a spade on dummy's ♣KQ.

East hand:
♠ J 3
♥ A
♦ J 9 8 7 6 5
♣ 9 7 6 5

South hand:
♠ Q 9 4
♥ K J 9 8 7 2
♦ 10 2
♣ A 4

Neither a spade continuation by West nor a club shift would beat 3♥.

You might question East's play of the ♠J when he didn't want a ruff; but if he played the three instead, West might carelessly but routinely continue with the ♠A since that play would look safe.

Dlr: East
Vul: Both

♠ 6 3
♥ K 10 4
♦ Q 6 5
♣ A K J 5 4

♠ 4
♥ Q 9 7 6 2
♦ K 10 7 2
♣ 9 7 2

WEST	NORTH	EAST	SOUTH
		Pass	Pass
Pass	1♣	1♠	2 NT
Pass	3 NT	All Pass	

Against 3NT, you risk a pithy comment from your partner by leading your long suit instead of his. (If your lead comes to grief, he may ask whether you would have led a spade if he had bid hearts.) Your ♥6 goes to dummy's king, East's ace and declarer's five. Back comes the ♥3, South follows with the eight and your queen wins.

How do you continue?

****

South's play at the first trick was odd. To play low from dummy would be normal, providing a chance for two heart tricks. Moreover, East was more likely to have the ♥A for his bid.

The likely explanation is that South was desperate to win the first trick because he feared a switch to another suit. That can only be diamonds, so you should lead the ♦2 at the third trick.

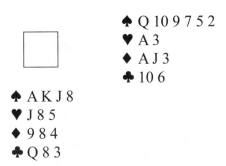

♠ Q 10 9 7 5 2
♥ A 3
♦ A J 3
♣ 10 6

♠ A K J 8
♥ J 8 5
♦ 9 8 4
♣ Q 8 3

South could, and perhaps should, have made 3NT by playing low from dummy on the opening lead. With East to lead to trick two, the defense could never take more than three fast diamond tricks.

Dlr: South   ♠ 5 2
Vul: Both   ♥ A Q 4 3
                  ♦ 10 7 3
                  ♣ A 10 6 2

♠ A 9 3
♥ 6 5
♦ K 9 8 6 4
♣ Q 9 4

WEST	NORTH	EAST	SOUTH
			1 NT
Pass	2♣	Pass	2♠
Pass	3 NT	All Pass	

You lead the ♦6: three, jack, queen. Declarer continues with the ♥K, ♥A and ♥Q, and you discard a spade. Next, he cashes the ♣A and leads a club to his jack and your queen.

How do you continue?

****

South started with three hearts and, on the auction, four spades. He must have four clubs to play the suit that way. If he had K-J-x, he would have led to his jack without cashing the ace, preserving communication.

If declarer's pattern was 4-3-2-4, you can safely lead a second low diamond to force out his ace.

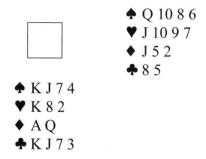

                    ♠ Q 10 8 6
                    ♥ J 10 9 7
                    ♦ J 5 2
                    ♣ 8 5

♠ K J 7 4
♥ K 8 2
♦ A Q
♣ K J 7 3

Declarer has only eight winners, and when you get in with the ♠A, you will run the diamonds for down one.

```
Dlr: East              ♠ 8 6 3
Vul: Both              ♥ 7 4 2
                       ♦ A 8 2
                       ♣ K J 6 4
♠ K Q 9 2
♥ J 10 6
♦ K 4              ┌────────┐
♣ A 9 7 2         │        │
                  │        │
                  └────────┘
```

WEST	NORTH	EAST	SOUTH
		Pass	Pass
1♣	Pass	1♠	2♦
2♠	3♦	All Pass	

You made a delicate decision to sell out to 3♦. At matchpoints, you would consider bidding 3♠. That would gain if 3♠ made or if you were down one (presumably undoubled) for -100 when South could have made 3♦ for +110. At IMPs, the goal on partscore deals is to be plus. Bidding 3♠ would gain only if both 3♠ and 3♦ made, and that seems unlikely.

You lead the ♠K, and East signals with the ten. He wins the next spade with the ace, South dropping the jack. South ruffs the third spade, leads a trump to the ace and returns a trump: jack, queen, king. You exit with the ♥J, and South wins with the king.

Next comes a club from South. Do you take your ace or duck? (Play promptly.)

****

You should have done your thinking in advance -- at the latest when you were in with the ♦K -- so you can take your ♣A.

South had six diamonds and two spades and must have held four hearts. If East had four, he would have responded 1♥ to your 1♣ opening, showing his four-card major suits "up the line." So South's club is a singleton.

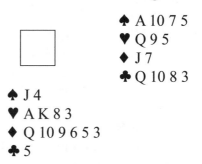

```
                          ♠ A 10 7 5
                          ♥ Q 9 5
         ┌────────┐       ♦ J 7
         │        │       ♣ Q 10 8 3
         └────────┘
         ♠ J 4
         ♥ A K 8 3
         ♦ Q 10 9 6 5 3
         ♣ 5
```

If you grab your ♣A, the defense will also get a heart for down one.

Dlr: North   ♠ 10 7 5
Vul: Both   ♥ J 10 7 5
         ♦ 8 6
         ♣ A 6 5 2

                        ♠ A 8 3
                        ♥ 9 6 4 2
                        ♦ A 5
                        ♣ K J 10 8

WEST	NORTH	EAST	SOUTH
	Pass	1♣	1♦
1♠	Pass	2♠	3♦
All Pass			

When you raised to 2♠, you thought it likely that West had a five-card suit; he probably has no more than five since he might have competed further with six. He leads the ♥K, which looks bad for the defense when South takes the ace. At the second trick, South leads the ♦K to your ace.

What do you lead to trick three?

****

How can you win five tricks? Even if two spade tricks are available, you may need a club. But if South had a club loser and needed to set up a discard promptly, why didn't he return a heart at the second trick?

Lead the ♥9, playing West for the ♥KQ doubleton and angling for a third-round ruff.

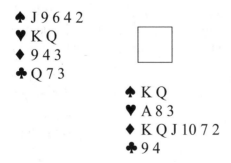

     ♠ J 9 6 4 2
     ♥ K Q
     ♦ 9 4 3
     ♣ Q 7 3

                 ♠ K Q
                 ♥ A 8 3
                 ♦ K Q J 10 7 2
                 ♣ 9 4

West will treat your ♥9 as suit preference and return a spade to your ace. After he ruffs your heart return, he will shift to a club, forcing out dummy's ace before the trumps are drawn, and South will have to lose another trick.

```
Dlr: South          ♠ A Q J 9 5
Vul: N-S            ♥ Q 4
                    ♦ K J 5
                    ♣ 10 6 2
     ♠ 8 4
     ♥ J 9 7 2          ┌───┐
     ♦ A 8 2            │   │
     ♣ A Q 8 3          └───┘
```

WEST	NORTH	EAST	SOUTH
			1♣
Pass	1♠	Pass	1 NT
Pass	3 NT	All Pass	

You lead the ♥2, dummy plays the four, East the ten and declarer wins with the ace. At trick two he leads the ♦4.

How do you defend?

****

Declarer is a favorite to hold both major-suit kings. If his heart holding were A-8-3 or A-8-5-3, he would have put up dummy's ♥Q at the first trick as the only chance to win a trick with it. If he lacked the ♠K, he would have attacked the spades at the second trick.

So declarer has eight tricks; a diamond will give him nine. You may as well take your ♦A. If South has a hand such as K103,AK63,974,K95, the contract is unbeatable even if you play low and he misguesses. You must assume that South has the ♦Q and weak clubs. After you take the ♦A, lead the ♣3.

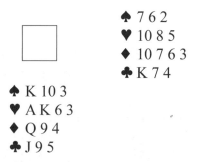

```
                    ♠ 7 6 2
     ┌───┐          ♥ 10 8 5
     │   │          ♦ 10 7 6 3
     └───┘          ♣ K 7 4
     ♠ K 10 3
     ♥ A K 6 3
     ♦ Q 9 4
     ♣ J 9 5
```

When East takes his ♣K, he should interpret your ♣3 -- a low club -- as showing interest in a club continuation rather than a shift back to hearts. If you wanted a heart return, you would lead a high club.

Dlr: East   ♠ K J 7 5 3
Vul: Both   ♥ Q 7
                  ♦ A Q 2
                  ♣ K 10 5

♠ A 6
♥ 10 8 5 4 2
♦ 8 7 6
♣ J 6 2

WEST	NORTH	EAST	SOUTH
		Pass	Pass
Pass	1♠	Pass	1 NT
All Pass			

Many players wouldn't open 1NT as North -- even if willing to suppress the five-card major -- because a transfer response by South might strand the partnership at a 5-2 heart fit when a 5-3 spade fit existed.

You lead the ♥4: queen, king. South ducks, ducks again when East returns the ♥J, and wins the third heart. He leads to the ♦Q and cashes the ace. East plays the nine and jack, and South overtakes with the king and leads the ♠2. How do you defend?

****

Declarer has five diamond tricks and one heart; he needs a black-suit trick to make 1NT. South can't have both black queens, which would give him 11 HCP for his 1NT response. If he has one black queen, which is it? Clearly, the ♠Q. If South had the ♣Q, he would lead a club to set up his seventh trick instead of subjecting himself to a guess in spades.

In that case (or if South has neither black queen), you should step in with your ♠A, cash two hearts and lead a club.

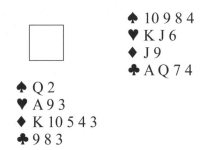

                   ♠ 10 9 8 4
                   ♥ K J 6
                   ♦ J 9
                   ♣ A Q 7 4

         ♠ Q 2
         ♥ A 9 3
         ♦ K 10 5 4 3
         ♣ 9 8 3

This type of problem is harder at the table than on paper. At low-level partscore contracts, the defenders often have more trouble placing the cards. Moreover, a defender must often make a crucial decision without a revealing hesitation.

I would sympathize with West if he ducked the ♠A, but only if he did so without a pause. Like most players, I find it easier to forgive a prompt error than a giveaway hitch.

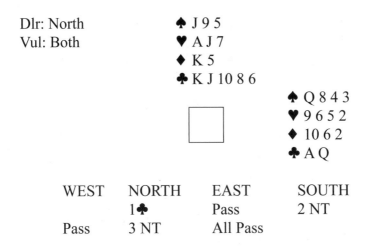

Dlr: North
Vul: Both

♠ J 9 5
♥ A J 7
♦ K 5
♣ K J 10 8 6

♠ Q 8 4 3
♥ 9 6 5 2
♦ 10 6 2
♣ A Q

WEST	NORTH	EAST	SOUTH
	1♣	Pass	2 NT
Pass	3 NT	All Pass	

West leads the ♠2, and dummy plays the jack. Presumably, you unhesitatingly cover with your queen ... or would you consider before you play?

****

South surely has a high spade. But then his normal play from dummy would be the nine. If the layout were

J95

K1062/Q1062   Q843/K843

A7

he could win a second spade trick.

If South is a capable declarer, you should refuse to cover. The defense will win three spades and two clubs if the West and South cards are

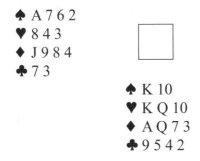

♠ A 7 6 2
♥ 8 4 3
♦ J 9 8 4
♣ 7 3

♠ K 10
♥ K Q 10
♦ A Q 7 3
♣ 9 5 4 2

When declarer played dummy's ♠J, he was coaxing you to cover and give away a trick.

Dlr: South   ♠ A 10 5 2
Vul: N-S   ♥ 7 3
        ♦ 8 5
        ♣ J 10 6 5 2

♠ K 8 3
♥ Q 9 5 2
♦ A Q 10 6 4
♣ 3

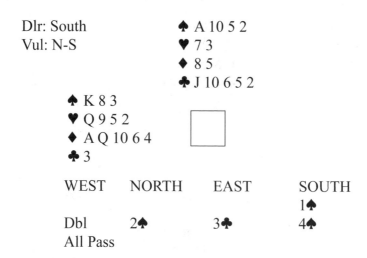

WEST	NORTH	EAST	SOUTH
			1♠
Dbl	2♠	3♣	4♠
All Pass			

I personally wouldn't dream of doubling 1♠ for takeout with that skinny West hand. The prospect of having partner bid clubs, clubs and more clubs would terrify me. But for the sake of the problem, assume that you survive and end up defending against 4♠.

You lead the ♣3, and East takes the ace and returns the nine. Declarer follows with the queen and king, and you ruff.

What do you lead at trick three?

****

East's ♣9 was a suit-preference play: his highest remaining club to suggest strength in hearts, the high-ranking side suit. Still, for you to lead a heart would be wrong. East has a fair hand, and if he had four cards in hearts, the suit for which your double of 1♠ implied good support, he would have bid hearts.

So South's pattern is likely to be 5-4-2-2. If he has a heart loser, it won't go away. South can discard two hearts on the ♣J10 but will still have two left.

However, South can effectively discard diamonds on the high clubs. Cash your ♦A, then lead a heart.

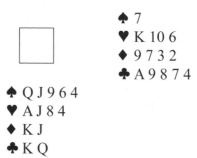

         ♠ 7
         ♥ K 10 6
         ♦ 9 7 3 2
         ♣ A 9 8 7 4

♠ Q J 9 6 4
♥ A J 8 4
♦ K J
♣ K Q

Dlr: South
Vul: Both

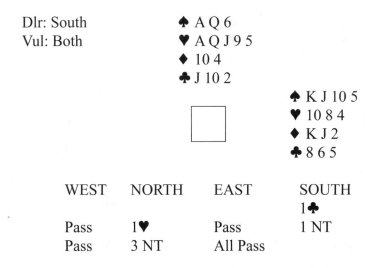

♠ A Q 6
♥ A Q J 9 5
♦ 10 4
♣ J 10 2

♠ K J 10 5
♥ 10 8 4
♦ K J 2
♣ 8 6 5

WEST	NORTH	EAST	SOUTH
			1♣
Pass	1♥	Pass	1 NT
Pass	3 NT	All Pass	

West gratifies you by leading the ♠8. Declarer considers the matter and plays the queen from dummy, losing to your king.

How do you continue?

****

West's opening lead marks declarer with the ♠9, so declarer could have gained time by playing low from dummy. It appears he is willing -- maybe eager -- for you to continue spades, hence you should consider a shift. Try the ♦J.

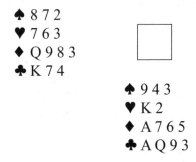

♠ 8 7 2
♥ 7 6 3
♦ Q 9 8 3
♣ K 7 4

♠ 9 4 3
♥ K 2
♦ A 7 6 5
♣ A Q 9 3

Your diamond shift will win five tricks for the defense. If instead you continue with the ♠J, South will take the ace and finesse in clubs, losing one club and three spades.

South could have succeeded by winning the first spade. He must have feared that you had five spades. His actual play would have worked against most defenders.

Dlr: South   ♠ K 4
Vul: N-S   ♥ Q J 3
                ♦ 9 6 5
                ♣ K Q J 5 4

♠ J 10 9 5
♥ K 5
♦ A Q 10 3
♣ 10 8 7

WEST	NORTH	EAST	SOUTH
			1♥
Pass	2♣	Pass	2♦
Pass	3♥	Pass	4♥
All Pass			

You lead the ♠J, won by dummy's king. Declarer then lets the ♥Q ride to your king.

What do you lead at the third trick?

****

You can't always see declarer's hand exactly, but you can visualize a hand for him that gives you two chances to beat the contract instead of one.

A club return will work if East has the ace but will result in overtricks if South has it. For an extra chance, lead the ♦3.

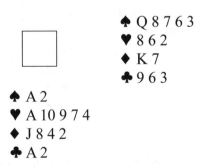

                              ♠ Q 8 7 6 3
                              ♥ 8 6 2
                              ♦ K 7
                              ♣ 9 6 3

♠ A 2
♥ A 10 9 7 4
♦ J 8 4 2
♣ A 2

You will also prevail with the diamond shift if declarer holds A2,A10974,KJ42,32 -- East will get in with the ♣A later and lead his last diamond -- or even if declarer holds A2,A10974,KJ742,2.

```
Dlr: South          ♠ A Q 6
Vul: Both           ♥ 10 7 5 4 2
                    ♦ A J 5 2
                    ♣ 7
                                    ♠ J 7 5
                                    ♥ A Q 8 3
                                    ♦ 9 4
                                    ♣ A J 8 2
```

WEST	NORTH	EAST	SOUTH
			1♦
Pass	1♥	Pass	2♣
Pass	3♦	Pass	3 NT
All Pass			

North's jump-preference was invitational, hence a slight underbid. (If South's hand is short in hearts, North's hand is mountainous.) Against 3NT, West leads the ♠2, and declarer plays dummy's queen, winning. At the second trick, dummy leads a club.

How do you defend?

****

Shelve the rule of playing "second hand low" and consider your defensive prospects. Surely South has the ♠K; he wouldn't have bid 3NT with three low spades. South should have five diamonds. If he had a hand such as K94,K6,K1076,KQ93, he wouldn't have treated his hand as a two-suiter; he would have rebid 1NT (and might well have opened 1♣). With K94,K6,KQ76,KQ93, he would have opened 1NT.

So South has eight tricks -- five diamonds and three spades -- and may be about to score another in clubs. But assuming his pattern is 3-1-5-4, you should rise with the ♣A and cash the ♥A.

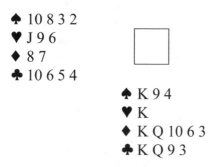

```
♠ 10 8 3 2
♥ J 9 6
♦ 8 7
♣ 10 6 5 4
                    ♠ K 9 4
                    ♥ K
                    ♦ K Q 10 6 3
                    ♣ K Q 9 3
```

West will unblock his nine, and you will take three more hearts for down one.

Dlr: North   ♠ J 10 6 5
Vul: Both   ♥ K 7 5
        ♦ K 8
        ♣ A K 8 5

♠ 3 2
♥ A 10 8 4 2
♦ J 5 3
♣ J 10 9

WEST	NORTH	EAST	SOUTH
	1♣	Pass	1♠
Pass	2♠	Pass	2 NT
Pass	4♠	All Pass	

You lead the ♣J, the king wins and East plays the deuce. When declarer next leads the ♠J from dummy, East wins with the king and shifts to the ♥9. South follows with the three.

South's second bid suggested about 11 points with balanced pattern. If East's ♥9 is a singleton, you must take your ace and return a heart; but if East had a doubleton heart, you need to duck.

What about it?

****

South probably has only four spades -- if East had the doubleton A-K, his defense would make no sense -- and if South had four hearts, his response to 1♣ would have been 1♥.

Signal with the ♥10. When East gets back in with the ♠A, he will lead his second heart, and you will win and give him a ruff for the setting trick.

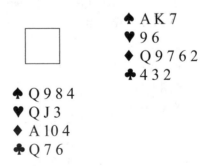

         ♠ A K 7
         ♥ 9 6
         ♦ Q 9 7 6 2
         ♣ 4 3 2

♠ Q 9 8 4
♥ Q J 3
♦ A 10 4
♣ Q 7 6

Another inference is present: If East had a singleton heart, he would have cashed his second high trump before leading his singleton, giving you no option but to win immediately and return a heart.

CHAPTER 10

More missing queens

If an inexperienced player faces a two-way guess for a queen, he may invoke "eight ever, nine never," which mandates playing to drop the queen with nine cards in a suit but finessing with fewer. Its validity is mathematically tenuous. With nine cards, the odds on playing for the drop are only about two percent better than guessing which way to finesse. If declarer has any clue at all, or just wants to rely on instinct, to finesse is defensible.

Of course, the best approach, which more seasoned players adopt, is to deduce the location of the queen using clues from the bidding, opening lead and later play.

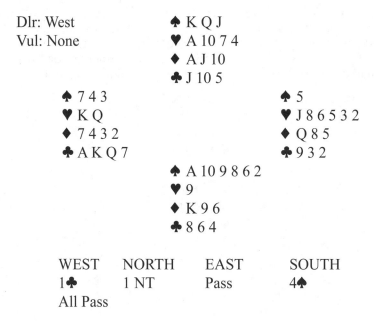

```
Dlr: West        ♠ K Q J
Vul: None        ♥ A 10 7 4
                 ♦ A J 10
                 ♣ J 10 5
♠ 7 4 3                        ♠ 5
♥ K Q                          ♥ J 8 6 5 3 2
♦ 7 4 3 2                      ♦ Q 8 5
♣ A K Q 7                      ♣ 9 3 2
                 ♠ A 10 9 8 6 2
                 ♥ 9
                 ♦ K 9 6
                 ♣ 8 6 4
```

WEST	NORTH	EAST	SOUTH
1♣	1 NT	Pass	4♠
All Pass			

North's 1NT overcall wouldn't suit everybody, but nowadays some players think stoppers are for children. West cashes three high clubs, to which East follows, and shifts to the ♥K. Declarer takes the ace and ruffs a heart, dropping the queen. He draws trumps and ruffs another heart, and West discards.

South knows that West had three spades, two hearts and four clubs. (With 3-2-5-3 pattern he would have opened 1♦.) So his pattern was balanced, and he has shown 14 HCP in hearts and clubs. If West had the ♦Q, what would his opening bid have been?

Dlr: West   ♠ A
Vul: None   ♥ A 10 7 6
Matchpoints   ♦ K Q 6 5
            ♣ A 10 5 2

♠ Q J 10 7 5 4 2		♠ 9 6
♥ 3		♥ Q 9 8
♦ 7 4 3		♦ A J 10 9
♣ K 4		♣ Q 8 7 6

            ♠ K 8 3
            ♥ K J 5 4 2
            ♦ 8 2
            ♣ J 9 3

WEST	NORTH	EAST	SOUTH
3♠	Dbl	Pass	4♥
All Pass			

West leads the ♠Q to dummy's ace. South should take the ♥A and finesse with the jack. (No "nine never" here.) East is likely to have heart length when West has great length in spades. Moreover, West is likely to have a singleton somewhere -- 7-2-2-2 pattern is the least attractive for a preempt -- and if he had a side-suit singleton, he probably would have led it.

Dlr: West   ♠ K 10 5
Vul: Both   ♥ K 6 4
            ♦ Q 10 6
            ♣ 8 5 4 3

            ♠ A J 9 7 3 2
            ♥ A Q J
            ♦ J 9 3
            ♣ J

WEST	NORTH	EAST	SOUTH
Pass	Pass	Pass	1♠
Pass	2♠	Pass	3♠
Pass	4♠	All Pass	

West leads the ♣2, and East takes the king and leads the ace, which you ruff. How do you play the trump suit?

****

East has a diamond honor. If West had the ♦AK, his opening lead would have been a high diamond. East might have opened with the ♣AK and ♦A but surely would have opened in third seat with Q6,932,K854,AK96. Play West for the ♠Q.

♠ Q 8 4		♠ 6
♥ 10 8 7		♥ 9 5 3 2
♦ A 7 2		♦ K 8 5 4
♣ Q 10 7 2		♣ A K 9 6

```
Dlr: East              ♠ K J 9 4
Vul: Both              ♥ 4 3 2
                       ♦ K 6 5
                       ♣ 7 6 5


                       ♠ A 10 6 5 2
                       ♥ K 6 5
                       ♦ 8 7
                       ♣ A K Q
```

WEST	NORTH	EAST	SOUTH
		Pass	1♠
Pass	2♠	Pass	3♠
All Pass			

A fit of optimism, brought on by the lure of a vulnerable game bonus, induces you to invite game. North rejects.

My practice is to stretch to invite vulnerable games, otherwise good games will be missed, but not to stretch to accept an invitation. With a sound invitation, opener should adopt the most practical game-try of all: "Bid game and try to make it." But I can understand the opposite approach -- invite soundly, accept aggressively -- that avoids going minus after a pushy invitation partner can't accept.

West leads the ♦2, and when you play low from dummy, East wins with the jack and shifts to the ♣10.

How do you play the trumps?

****

West probably has the ♦Q, but East has the ♦AJ, and you must assume that he has the ♥A to have a chance. Moreover, if West had the ♥QJ, he would have led the ♥Q instead of a diamond from a broken holding. Since many if not most Easts would open on Q3,AJ,AJ93,109842, you should play West for the ♠Q.

```
    ♠ Q 7 3              ♠ 8
    ♥ Q 10 8 7           ♥ A J 9
    ♦ Q 10 4 2           ♦ A J 9 3
    ♣ J 3                ♣ 10 9 8 4 2
```

Dlr: South
Vul: N-S

♠ A 6 4 2
♥ 10 4 2
♦ A J 5
♣ J 9 8

♠ 7 3
♥ A K J 3
♦ 2
♣ A Q 10 7 6 4

WEST	NORTH	EAST	SOUTH
			1♣
1♠	1 NT	2♦	2♥
2♠	4♣	Pass	5♣
All Pass			

North thought your 2♥ bid showed substantial extra strength, hence his jump to 4♣; but the resulting 5♣ contract is fair enough.

West leads the ♠K. You take dummy's ace and pass the ♣9, losing to the king. West cashes the ♠Q, East discarding the ♦10, and shifts to the ♦Q. You take dummy's ace, ruff a diamond high, go back to the ♣8 -- East throws a diamond -- and ruff a diamond high. West discards a spade. You draw West's last trump with dummy's jack.

How do you play the hearts?

****

You have a count. West started with six spades, three clubs and two diamonds, so two hearts. A finesse with the ♥J won't help you even if it wins; East's Q-x-x-x will still be worth a trick.

Take the ♥AK, hoping West has Q-x.

♠ K Q J 9 8 5   ♠ 10
♥ Q 7   ♥ 9 8 6 5
♦ Q 4   ♦ K 10 9 8 7 6 3
♣ K 3 2   ♣ 5

Dlr: West   ♠ A 5
Vul: None   ♥ K 10 8
                 ♦ Q 6 5
                 ♣ J 7 6 4 2

                 ♠ 9 2
                 ♥ A J 9 7 5 2
                 ♦ 8 2
                 ♣ A K 10

WEST	NORTH	EAST	SOUTH
1♠	Pass	2♠	3♥
Pass	4♥	All Pass	

West leads the ♣4 to dummy's ace. How do you attack the trump suit?

****

West, who opened the bidding, is more likely to have the ♥Q, but logic indicates that he almost surely has it. Judging from the opening lead, East has a spade honor and also has a diamond honor: West would have laid down a high diamond with the king and ace.

Play West for the ♥Q.

♠ K J 8 4 3	♠ Q 10 7 6
♥ Q 6 3	♥ 4
♦ A J 7	♦ K 10 9 4 3
♣ Q 5	♣ 9 8 3

After you pick up the trumps, you will play West for the ♣Q on the same reasoning.

The modern tendency to open light hands can impede one's own constructive bidding, but it often gains by facilitating competition. Moreover, if West were a light opener, South could not reliably draw the same inferences about the location of the missing queens.

Many players would have bid more as East.

	♠ K J 7
Dlr: South	♥ Q 10 3
Vul: Both	♦ A 10 7
	♣ K J 9 4

♠ A Q 10 8 4 2
♥ A J 6
♦ 5
♣ A 10 3

WEST	NORTH	EAST	SOUTH
			1♠
Pass	2 NT	Pass	6♠
All Pass			

After a highly scientific auction, West leads the ♦K against your slam. You take the ace and correctly set out to get information. You ruff a diamond, lead to the ♣J, ruff a diamond and draw trumps with the ♠A and ♠K. West follows, East throws a club and a diamond. Both opponents have followed low to the diamond plays.

Next you let the ♥Q ride, and West takes the king and returns a heart. When you take the ♥AJ, East discards another club.

Who has the ♣Q?

****

West started with three trumps and five hearts. He had at least four diamonds: He led the king and followed low when you ruffed diamonds, so he still has the queen. Lead a club to the king. If the queen doesn't come up from West, return a club to your ten.

♠ 9 5 3		♠ 6
♥ K 8 7 5 2		♥ 9 4
♦ K Q 9 6		♦ J 8 4 3 2
♣ 2		♣ Q 8 7 6 5

```
Dlr: West          ♠ J 7 4
Vul: Both          ♥ K Q J 3
                   ♦ A 9 3
                   ♣ K 7 4


                   ♠ Q 10 5
                   ♥ A 9 5 4 2
                   ♦ K J 8
                   ♣ 5 3
```

WEST	NORTH	EAST	SOUTH
1♣	Dbl	Pass	2♥
Pass	2 NT	Pass	4♥
All Pass			

North's decision to move on over South's invitational jump to 2♥ was close. North's ♥J was probably a wasted point -- South could draw trumps without it -- but the ♣K was worth as much as an ace.

West leads the ♣A and continues with the ♣Q. Dummy's king wins, and East follows with the six and eight. You draw trumps with the king, queen and jack; West had the singleton ten.

How do you play the diamonds?

****

The high spades are surely split: If West had the king and ace, he would have led or shifted to a high spade. Suppose you confirm that by leading a spade to the jack. East takes the ace and returns a club, and you ruff and lead a second spade. West wins and exits with a third spade to your queen.

West needs the ♦Q for his opening bid; if he doesn't have it, he has opened with 10 HCP. Your best chance, given that West has some length in diamonds, is a backward finesse. Lead the ♦J. When West covers, take dummy's ace and return a diamond to your eight.

```
♠ K 9 6 3              ♠ A 8 2
♥ 10                   ♥ 8 7 6
♦ Q 5 2                ♦ 10 7 6 4
♣ A Q J 9 2            ♣ 10 8 6
```

Dlr: South   ♠ J 3
Vul: Both   ♥ 8 7 6
                     ♦ Q J
                     ♣ K J 10 9 6 3

                     ♠ A K Q
                     ♥ A K Q 4
                     ♦ 5 4 2
                     ♣ A 8 4

WEST	NORTH	EAST	SOUTH
			2 NT
Pass	3 NT	All Pass	

The bidding is unexceptional, but the contract is scary, even after West leads the ♠2. You win with the ace and cash your three high hearts; a 3-3 split will give you nine tricks, but West discards a diamond.

How do you play the clubs?

****

West had four spades, from his lead of the deuce, and two hearts. If he had a five-card diamond suit, he would have preferred to lead that suit after the auction you had. Give West 4-2-4-3 or 4-2-3-4 pattern. Cash the ♣A, planning to finesse with the jack next.

       ♠ 10 7 6 2   ♠ 9 8 5 4
       ♥ 10 3   ♥ J 9 5 2
       ♦ 10 8 6 3   ♦ A K 9 7
       ♣ Q 7 2   ♣ 5

(Winning play attributed to Zia.)

Dlr: South ♠ J 10
Vul: Both   ♥ K 7 6 4
            ♦ K 10 3 2
            ♣ Q J 5

            ♠ K Q 5 4
            ♥ A Q 3
            ♦ A 7 4
            ♣ A K 8

WEST	NORTH	EAST	SOUTH
			2 NT
Pass	4 NT	Pass	6 NT
All Pass			

You have only 32 HCP to work with. If dummy had one more club and one fewer diamond, 6NT would be cold. As it is, your club honors aren't carrying their weight.

West leads the ♠9, and East takes the ace and returns a spade to dummy's jack. You cash three rounds of clubs, East-West following, and next the king, ace and queen of hearts. West discards the ♦5. When you take the ♠KQ, West follows. Dummy throws a diamond and a heart, and East discards the ♥J.

At the 11th trick, you cash your ♦A: six, three, jack. On the next diamond, West plays the nine. Do you finesse with dummy's ten or put up the king?

****

If you have been counting, you know what to do. West had four spades, two hearts and three or four clubs, hence no more than four diamonds. East had at least two diamomds.

Put up the ♦K.

    ♠ 9 8 7 6   ♠ A 3 2
    ♥ 10 5   ♥ J 9 8 2
    ♦ 9 8 6 5   ♦ Q J
    ♣ 9 4 3   ♣ 10 7 6 2

(Winning play attributed to the late Meyer Schleifer.)

```
Dlr: East          ♠ 10 8 2
Vul: Both          ♥ 5 2
                   ♦ K 8 5
                   ♣ A J 7 5 3


                   ♠ A K J 9 5
                   ♥ A K 8
                   ♦ J 10 9 2
                   ♣ 10
```

WEST	NORTH	EAST	SOUTH
		1♥	1♠
Pass	2♣	Pass	4♠
All Pass			

They always find the best defense against you. West leads the ♦7, and East takes the queen and ace and leads a third diamond. West ruffs and leads the ♥3.

You take the ♥AK and cash the ♠A. Both defenders play low. Next, suppose you mark time by leading to the ♣A and ruffing a club. East drops the ♣K, then discards a heart. When you ruff your third heart in dummy, both defenders follow. On the trump return, East plays low.

Do you go up with the ♠K or finesse?

****

You should finesse. East started with five hearts, four diamonds and one club, hence three spades.

```
♠ 6 3                      ♠ Q 7 4
♥ 10 7 3                   ♥ Q J 9 6 4
♦ 7 3                      ♦ A Q 6 4
♣ Q 9 8 6 4 2              ♣ K
```

Even if you forget to get a distributional count by testing the clubs, you should still make 4♠ by taking the trump finesse. You can infer that West would not make a speculative opening lead, trying for a ruff, if he held ♠Qxx -- a probable trump trick anyway.

```
Dlr: West            ♠ A 3 2
Vul: Both            ♥ A 9 4
                     ♦ Q 4 2
                     ♣ K J 8 6


                     ♠ K 6 5
                     ♥ K Q 10 8 5
                     ♦ 7 6 5
                     ♣ A 7
```

WEST	NORTH	EAST	SOUTH
Pass	1♣	Pass	1♥
Dbl	Pass	1♠	2♠
Pass	3♥	Pass	4♥
All Pass			

Your auction misfired. North could have bid 2NT at his third turn; you could have tried 3NT at yours.

Against 4♥, West leads the ♦K, ♦A and a third diamond. East follows with the jack and nine, ruffs dummy's queen and shifts to the ♠9. You win with the king, and West follows with the four. Next you take the ♥KA, finding that West had J-7.

How do you continue?

****

You need a pitch for your spade loser and can't hope to win a finesse with the ♣J. West didn't open the bidding, and he is marked with 11 HCP: ♦AK, ♠QJ, ♥J.

Lead the ♣J through East. When he covers, take the ace and lead a second club. On the bidding, West almost surely has only two clubs. (East was obliged to bid 1♠ with a three-card holding.) You must hope West has 10-x or 9-x.

```
♠ Q J 10 4          ♠ 9 8 7
♥ J 7               ♥ 6 3 2
♦ A K 10 8 3        ♦ J 9
♣ 9 3               ♣ Q 10 5 4 2
```

As the cards lie, you can take the ♣K and return the eight for a winning ruffing finesse through East.

```
Dlr: East          ♠ J 10 6 4
Vul: N-S           ♥ J 5
                   ♦ A K 4 2
                   ♣ K Q J


                   ♠ A K 9 8 3
                   ♥ Q 7 6 2
                   ♦ J 5
                   ♣ 10 6
```

WEST	NORTH	EAST	SOUTH
		1♥	Pass
Pass	Dbl	Pass	1♠
Pass	2♠	Pass	3♠
Pass	4♠	All Pass	

If North had doubled 1♥ in the direct position, he would have passed a minimum response by South; but after North's balancing double, which could have been shaded, he raised to 2♠ to show a sound hand.

West leads the ♥4. East takes the king and ace, and West follows with the three. Next, East cashes the ♣A and leads a second club to dummy.

How do you play the trump suit?

****

Unless East is out to lunch, your play is clearly indicated. If West had the ♠Q, East could have beaten the contract by leading a third heart, letting his partner ruff ahead of dummy. That would be a marked defense since East could expect no more side-suit tricks except his ♣A.

Since it didn't happen, lead a trump to your ace, go back to dummy with a high diamond and return the ♠J, intending to finesse.

```
        ♠ 7                        ♠ Q 5 2
        ♥ 4 3                      ♥ A K 10 9 8
        ♦ Q 9 8 7 3                ♦ 10 6
        ♣ 8 7 5 4 2                ♣ A 9 3
```

Dlr: West
Vul: N-S

     ♠ 9 6
     ♥ A 4 3 2
     ♦ J 3 2
     ♣ Q 4 3 2

     ♠ K Q J 10 8 7 2
     ♥ K J 5
     ♦ 5 4
     ♣ A

WEST	NORTH	EAST	SOUTH
1♦	Pass	Pass	4♠
All Pass			

West leads the ♦K and continues with the ace and queen. East follows, and you ruff and lead the ♠K. East takes the ace and returns a trump, and you draw trumps. West discards a diamond and a club.

How do you continue?

****

To finesse with the ♥J can't be right. East couldn't respond to the opening bid and has shown an ace, so West has the ♥Q. To try to drop the queen would be better than a hopeless finesse, but the best play is to run all your trumps. West, who is marked with the ♣K as well, will be squeezed in the end, unable to keep his ♣K plus a guard to the ♥Q.

♠ 3
♥ Q 10 6
♦ A K Q 7 6
♣ K J 6 5

♠ A 5 4
♥ 9 8 7
♦ 10 9 8
♣ 10 9 8 7

Dummy's last three cards will be the ♥A4 and ♣Q, and you will keep the ♥KJ5. If West doesn't discard his ♣K, you will play the ♥AK.

```
Dlr: East          ♠ A 6
Vul: None          ♥ K 10 4 3
                   ♦ 8 5 4
                   ♣ K 6 5 4


                   ♠ K 10 5
                   ♥ A J 9 6 2
                   ♦ Q 9
                   ♣ A 3 2
```

WEST	NORTH	EAST	SOUTH
		Pass	1♥
2♦	3♥	Pass	4♥
All Pass			

West cashes the ♦KA and continues with the jack. East discards the ♠2, and you ruff. You take the ♠AK and ruff a spade in dummy: West follows with the three, nine and jack, East with the four, seven and eight.

Next you take the ♣A and lead a second club. West follows (if he started with a singleton, he couldn't gain by ruffing a loser), and dummy's king wins.

How do you play the trumps?

****

You know West had at least 11 cards outside the trump suit. Cash the ♥K and lead a second heart, intending to finesse if East plays low. If West can win, he will have only diamonds left to lead, and you will ruff with dummy's last trump and discard your losing club.

```
♠ J 9 3                    ♠ Q 8 7 4 2
♥ Q 5                      ♥ 8 7
♦ A K J 10 7 3             ♦ 6 2
♣ 9 8                      ♣ Q J 10 7
```

Although the focus in this book is on counting and inference, "guesses" for a missing queen can involve techniques such as safety plays, avoidance, trump control, squeeze play (as in the previous deal) and endplays (as in this deal).

```
Dlr: South          ♠ 9 5 3
Vul: N-S            ♥ K J 6 4
                    ♦ A 10 4
                    ♣ 6 5 3


                    ♠ K Q 10 6 4
                    ♥ A 5 2
                    ♦ K J 3
                    ♣ K 4
```

WEST	NORTH	EAST	SOUTH
			1♠
Pass	2♠	Pass	3♠
Pass	4♠	All Pass	

You bid another hungry game, against which West leads the ♠2. East takes the ace and shifts to the ♣Q. Your king loses to West, and his club return goes to East's ten. You ruff the next club and take the ♠KQ, finding that West began with J-7-2. East discards a club.

Next, you cash the ♥A and lead a second heart toward dummy. West plays the ten and queen, and you gratefully take the king and jack. West discards a diamond.

Now you must guess right in diamonds. Who has the queen?

****

It's not clear, but indications exist. After your tentative auction to game, West would look for a passive opening lead. An aggressive lead from a queen or a king wouldn't appeal to him when both dummy and declarer suggested limited high-card strength.

West's lead from J-7-2 of trumps wasn't completely safe; it could have blown a trick on some layouts. If West had a hand such as J72,Q10,9875,A982, I would be willing to bet that he would have led a diamond.

Play West for the ♦Q.

```
♠ J 7 2            ♠ A 8
♥ Q 10             ♥ 9 8 7 3
♦ Q 9 8 2          ♦ 7 6 5
♣ A 9 8 2          ♣ Q J 10 7
```

Dlr: West
Vul: E-W

	♠ K 10 7 5 3
	♥ Q 8 5 2
	♦ Q 5 4
	♣ 7

♠ A J 2
♥ J 10 9 6 4 3
♦ 3
♣ A J 8

WEST	NORTH	EAST	SOUTH
Pass	Pass	1 NT	2♥
Pass	4♥	All Pass	

East's 1NT showed 16 to 18 HCP. West leads the ♦9, and East wins with the ten and tries to cash the king. You ruff and lead a trump. West follows low, and East takes the king and ace and leads the ♦A. You ruff again.

Who has the ♠Q?

****

You have seen East play 15 HCP. He has one more honor somewhere but can't have two. But if West had the ♣KQ, his opening lead would surely have been the ♣K, not a diamond from a worthless holding.

So you can place East with a club honor. Therefore, West has the ♠Q.

♠ Q 4	♠ 9 8 6
♥ 7	♥ A K
♦ 9 8 7 6 2	♦ A K J 10
♣ K 9 5 3 2	♣ Q 10 6 4

CHAPTER 11

Jack and king-jack guesses

I recall playing in an NABC event against the storied partnership of Edgar Kaplan and Norman Kay. As declarer, I led toward a king-jack combination and had to guess what to play. Kay, sitting behind me, held the ace and queen. After I had pondered for a few moments, he said, not unkindly, "Guess this one."

A guess for a jack, or a guess between playing a king or a jack, often yields to counting, inference and assumption. The hitch is that declarer will be doomed if the A-Q lie behind the K-J. Still, he should take his best shot at forming a picture of the missing hands based on the usual sources of information.

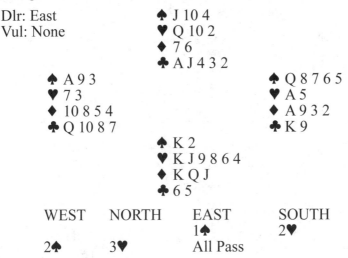

Dlr: East
Vul: None

♠ J 10 4
♥ Q 10 2
♦ 7 6
♣ A J 4 3 2

♠ A 9 3
♥ 7 3
♦ 10 8 5 4
♣ Q 10 8 7

♠ Q 8 7 6 5
♥ A 5
♦ A 9 3 2
♣ K 9

♠ K 2
♥ K J 9 8 6 4
♦ K Q J
♣ 6 5

WEST	NORTH	EAST	SOUTH
		1♠	2♥
2♠	3♥	All Pass	

West leads a trump, and East takes the ace and shifts to a spade. East opened the bidding and has most of the missing high cards, but the opening lead is telling. If West held Q-x-x or x-x-x in spades, why wouldn't he lead the suit his side bid and raised? But he might be reluctant to lead the ace. (The deal demonstrates why.)

Declarer should play West for the ♠A, East for the queen.

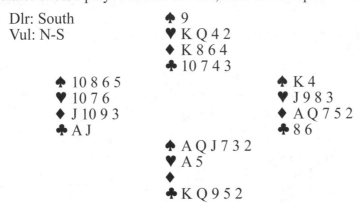

Dlr: South
Vul: N-S

♠ 9
♥ K Q 4 2
♦ K 8 6 4
♣ 10 7 4 3

♠ 10 8 6 5
♥ 10 7 6
♦ J 10 9 3
♣ A J

♠ K 4
♥ J 9 8 3
♦ A Q 7 5 2
♣ 8 6

♠ A Q J 7 3 2
♥ A 5
♦ —
♣ K Q 9 5 2

WEST	NORTH	EAST	SOUTH
			1♠
Pass	1 NT	Pass	3♣
Pass	4♣	Pass	6♣
All Pass			

West leads the ♦J, and declarer ruffs, He takes the ♠A and ruffs a spade in dummy. When East's king falls, declarer leads a trump to his king and West's ace. Declarer ruffs the diamond return. Next, he should plunk down the ♣Q. To enter dummy to finesse for the ♣J can't be right if West is awake. If East had the ♣J, West would have led a third spade, letting his partner overruff dummy.

Dlr: South	♠ J 6 4
Vul: N-S	♥ K 6 4
	♦ J 8 2
	♣ K J 8 2

	♠ A K Q 8 3
	♥ A 7 2
	♦ K Q 4
	♣ 5 3

WEST	NORTH	EAST	SOUTH
			1♠
Pass	2♠	Pass	4♠
All Pass			

West leads the ♥Q. You win with the king and draw trumps. West must discard three times. He lets go a heart and two clubs. You lead the ♦K to East's ace, win the heart return, and take the ♦J and ♦Q. Both defenders follow low.

Unable to delay any longer, you lead a club. West plays low. King or jack?

****

Play West for the ♣A. If he had, say, Q-10-x-x, he would have been reluctant to pitch any clubs, possibly conceding an extra trick.

♠ 9	♠ 10 7 5 2
♥ Q J 10 5	♥ 9 8 3
♦ 10 7 5 3	♦ A 9 6
♣ A 7 6 4	♣ Q 10 9

Dlr: East   ♠ J 7 6 5 2
Vul: None   ♥ J 7 5
             ♦ 6 3 2
             ♣ K J

             ♠ A K
             ♥ A Q 10 9 6 2
             ♦ A 10 5
             ♣ 7 5

WEST	NORTH	EAST	SOUTH
		Pass	1♥
Pass	2♥	Pass	4♥
All Pass			

West leads the ♦9, and East plays the jack. You take the ace and lead a club, and West plays low.

King or jack?

****

West's top-of-nothing opening lead marks East with the missing diamond honors, and you must hope he also has the ♥K. But East never bid. If you play the ♣J, you will probably go down even if it forces out the ace, losing a trump to West's king and two diamonds. Make a "second-degree assumption" and play the ♣K. Give yourself a chance.

♠ Q 9 8 3	♠ 10 4
♥ 4	♥ K 8 3
♦ 9 8 7	♦ K Q J 4
♣ A 10 8 4 3	♣ Q 9 6 2

Dlr: West   ♠ J 9 3
Vul: None   ♥ K 7 5 2
                  ♦ A Q 4
                  ♣ Q 9 4

                  ♠ 8 6
                  ♥ A J 10 9 6 3
                  ♦ 5 2
                  ♣ K 10 3

WEST	NORTH	EAST	SOUTH
1 NT	Pass	2♦	2♥
Pass	4♥	All Pass	

West's 1NT showed 16 to 18 HCP; East's 2♦ was natural and terminal.

Your 2♥ was a "pre-balance." When both opponents have limited values, you may enter the auction directly with a good suit but fewer values than normal. If you pass, your partner may not be able to balance. In light of that, North might have given you some room and raised to only 3♥.

Against 4♥, West leads the ♠K and continues with the ace and queen. You ruff and take the ♥A. When both defenders follow low, you finesse successfully with the ♦Q, cash the ♥K and ♦A, and ruff dummy's last diamond. West had the ♥Q4 and follows to the diamonds with the three, jack and king.

How do you play the clubs?

****

West has shown 15 HCP: ♠AKQ, ♥Q, ♦KJ. He can't have the ♣A but must have the ♣J. Lead the ♣10 and let it ride if West doesn't cover.

     ♠ A K Q 4   ♠ 10 7 5 2
     ♥ Q 4   ♥ 8
     ♦ K J 3   ♦ 10 9 8 7 6
     ♣ J 7 5 2   ♣ A 8 6

```
Dlr: East           ♠ A J 9 7
Vul: N-S            ♥ 7 5 3
                    ♦ K J 5
                    ♣ A Q 6


                    ♠ Q 10 8 6 3
                    ♥ A K 2
                    ♦ 4
                    ♣ J 10 7 3
```

WEST	NORTH	EAST	SOUTH
		Pass	Pass
Pass	1♣	Pass	1♠
Pass	2♠	Pass	4♠
All Pass			

West leads the ♥J to your king. The contract looks promising, but you have a potential loser in each suit. If the defenders get in, they will lead a second heart, setting up a winner, so you must try to establish a discard for your heart loser quickly.

When you lead a diamond at trick two, West plays low. King or jack?

****

Play the ♦K. East couldn't open the bidding and has the ♥Q. If he has the ♦A, you won't get your heart discard, but since one of the black-suit finesses will win, you will make the contract anyway.

```
    ♠ 4 2              ♠ K 5
    ♥ J 10 9 6         ♥ Q 8 4
    ♦ A 10 8 6         ♦ Q 9 7 3 2
    ♣ 8 4 2            ♣ K 9 5
```

```
Dlr: North              ♠ A K J
Vul: Both               ♥ K J 3 2
                        ♦ Q 7 5 3
                        ♣ A 10


                        ♠ Q 10 9 8 4
                        ♥ 6 5
                        ♦ 9 4
                        ♣ K Q 5 3
```

WEST	NORTH	EAST	SOUTH
	1♦	Pass	1♠
Pass	2 NT	Pass	3♣
Pass	3♠	Pass	4♠
All Pass			

West leads the ♣9: ten, jack, king.

Suppose you lead a heart at the second trick. This play may be psychologically effective. West knows from the bidding that your hand may be short in a red suit. If he thinks you have a singleton heart, you may induce him to rise with the ♥A and save you a guess.

But as it is, West follows smoothly with the ♥4. King or jack?

*****6****

If you're willing to assume that West might have been impelled to take the ♥A if he had it, play the jack from dummy. But an inference exists from the opening lead: On the auction, to lead the unbid suit would have been attractive, but West would have been more apt to lead a heart from the queen than to lay down the ♥A. Against a capable West, I would be inclined to put up the ♥K.

```
♠ 753              ♠ 62
♥ A974             ♥ Q 10 8
♦ K J 2            ♦ A 10 8 6
♣ 9 8 7            ♣ J 6 4 2
```

Ask yourself what West's opening lead would have been from 753,Q974,KJ2,987.

Dlr: West   ♠ Q 10 6 5 2
Vul: None   ♥ Q 7 3
                 ♦ 7 2
                 ♣ A Q 4

                 ♠ A K J 9 4
                 ♥ 9 8 4
                 ♦ K J 10
                 ♣ 6 3

WEST	NORTH	EAST	SOUTH
1♥	Pass	1 NT	2♠
Pass	3♠	All Pass	

West leads the ♥K. East signals with the jack, so West continues with the ♥A and a third heart, ruffed. Inevitably, East returns the ♦5.

King or jack?

****

Two pertinent high cards are missing: the ♦A and ♣K. East must have one of them for his 1NT response, and West has the other for his opening bid. But you need West to have the ♣K to have a chance. Play East for the ♦A.

    ♠ 7   ♠ 8 3
    ♥ A K 10 5 2   ♥ J 6
    ♦ Q 8 4   ♦ A 9 6 5 3
    ♣ K 10 7 5   ♣ J 9 8 2

At matchpoints, the problem would be less straightforward. The goal would be to beat the other pairs at 3♠, not to make the contract: A misguess in diamonds might cost a second undertrick and a lot of matchpoints. If an average West led the ♥10 at the third trick -- suit preference, suggesting a diamond entry -- declarer might elect to place him with the ♦A and play for down one.

Dlr: East
Vul: Both

♠ J 4
♥ J 9 3
♦ J 6 4
♣ 10 9 8 5 2

♠ K 10 3
♥ A K Q 10 4
♦ Q
♣ K J 7 4

WEST	NORTH	EAST	SOUTH
		1♠	Dbl
2♠	Pass	Pass	4♥
All Pass			

Your jump to 4♥ was bold, but you don't need much help in dummy to have a play. You expect a spade opening lead, your ♠K will be a winner and you can probably ruff your third spade in dummy.

West duly leads the ♠9, and East takes the ace and returns a spade. You win with dummy's jack and draw trumps with the ace, king and jack. East discards a spade. Next you lead the ♣10, and East plays the six.

Do you finesse or put up the king?

****

If East had the ♦AK, he would have led a high diamond at the second trick. If West has one high diamond, East needs the ♣A for his opening bid. Put up the ♣K.

♠ 9 8 2   ♠ A Q 7 6 5
♥ 8 5 2   ♥ 7 6
♦ A 10 7 5 2   ♦ K 9 8 3
♣ Q 3   ♣ A 6

To let the ♣10 ride would be right if East had A-Q-6, but then West could have beaten the contract easily by leading his singleton (and East could have beaten it by winning the first club and exiting safely).

Dlr: South   ♠ A 6
Vul: Both   ♥ A J 9 8
                ♦ K 10 8 4
                ♣ K 8 4

                ♠ K 8 2
                ♥ K Q 10 6 2
                ♦ Q 7 2
                ♣ A 5

WEST	NORTH	EAST	SOUTH
			1♥
1♠	2♣	Pass	2 NT
Pass	3♥	Pass	4♣
Pass	6♥	All Pass	

West leads the ♠Q, You take the ace and draw trumps, finding East with a singleton.

To make the slam, you must handle the diamonds. West surely has the ace for his vulnerable overcall, but the position of the jack is unknown. How do you continue?

****

Test the other suits. Cash the ♠K, ruff your last spade in dummy, take the ♣AK and ruff a club. East follows to the spades, and West follows to the clubs with the six, jack and queen. Now what's your view in diamonds?

****

West had five spades, three trumps and at least three clubs. Lead a diamond to the king and play low from your hand on the next diamond.

♠ Q J 10 9 5   ♠ 7 4 3
♥ 7 4 3   ♥ 5
♦ A 5   ♦ J 9 6 3
♣ Q J 6   ♣ 10 9 7 3 2

If your investigation found West with, say, 5-3-3-2 distribution, you would have other options.

```
Dlr: North          ♠ K J
Vul: N-S            ♥ Q 9 3 2
                   ♦ K J
                   ♣ 7 6 5 4 2


                   ♠ 7 6 4
                   ♥ A J 10 8 6
                   ♦ 9 5 2
                   ♣ A K
```

WEST	NORTH	EAST	SOUTH
	Pass	Pass	1♥
Pass	3♥	Pass	4♥
All Pass			

Confident of your guessing powers, you push on to game over North's limit raise. West leads the ♣J to your ace. This time you have a pair of K-J guesses plus a problem in trumps. Suppose you lead a diamond at the second trick, and West plays low.

King or jack?

****

Since West led the ♣J, East has the ♣Q. How should you place the other missing honors?

You could play West for a hand such as Q953,K4,Q10843,J10 or A953,K4,Q10843,J10. But it is best to make no more assumptions than necessary. Assume only that East has the ♥K, and the trump finesse will win. Then you will need to guess right in spades or diamonds but not in both suits -- and East won't have both aces since he would have opened the bidding.

Play the ♦K. If it wins, finesse in trumps. If you pick up the trumps, it's your day. With your luck, you'll probably guess right in spades too and make an overtrick.

Say the ♦K wins but the trump finesse loses, and West then leads a low spade. Finesse with dummy's jack. If West had a hand such as A953,K4,A10832,J10, he probably would have acted over your 1♥.

Backtracking, suppose East takes the ♦A at trick two and returns a diamond to West's queen. If West then leads a low spade, play the king from dummy. If East has the ace, you may go down two; but you probably weren't making the contract since West will have the ♥K.

```
    ♠ Q 9 5 3              ♠ A 10 8 2
    ♥ 7 4                  ♥ K 5
    ♦ A 10 8 4 3           ♦ Q 7 6
    ♣ J 10                 ♣ Q 9 8 3
```

Dlr: West ♠ Q 10 4
Vul: N-S ♥ J 5 4
  ♦ K Q
  ♣ K J 9 8 4

  ♠ A K J 9 2
  ♥ Q 8 3
  ♦ A J 4
  ♣ 6 3

WEST	NORTH	EAST	SOUTH
Pass	Pass	Pass	1♠
Pass	2♣	Pass	2 NT
Pass	3♠	Pass	4♠
All Pass			

West leads the ♦10. Planning to pitch a heart from dummy on the third diamond and try for a heart ruff in dummy is impractical; you might get stuck over there without a chance to make a club play. You must guess the clubs anyway, so say you win the first diamond with the ace and lead a club. West plays the deuce.

King or jack?

****

This looks like a clean guess. West would not have been tempted to take his ♣A for fear of losing it; he would play you for a doubleton club for your 2NT bid. Still, put up the ♣K. Part of the time, East will hold the ♥AK, and in those cases he won't have the ♣A since it would have given him a third-position opening bid.

♠ 8 5 3	♠ 7 6
♥ 9 7 6	♥ A K 10 2
♦ 10 9 8	♦ 7 6 5 3 2
♣ A 10 5 2	♣ Q 7

When the ♣K wins, you lose a club to East's queen. If he returns a trump (perhaps with a hand different from the one shown), win in dummy, ruff a club, return a diamond to dummy and ruff a club with the ♠K. Then you can take the ♠A and ♦J, draw the last missing trump in dummy, and cash the good fifth club for your 10th trick.

```
Dlr: South            ♠ 9 4 2
Vul: Both             ♥ K 5 3
                      ♦ K 5
                      ♣ 10 7 5 4 2


                      ♠ Q J 10 8 7 3
                      ♥ A Q 10 2
                      ♦ Q 7
                      ♣ A
```

WEST	NORTH	EAST	SOUTH
			1♠
Pass	2♠	Pass	4♠
All Pass			

West does part of your work for you by leading the ♠KA and a third spade. East discards a diamond and a club. You next cash the ♣A and lead a diamond to the king. East takes the ace and unhelpfully returns a diamond to your queen.

You cash your remaining trumps, but neither defender pitches a heart. When you take the ♥AK, they both follow low. On the third heart, East plays the nine.

Do you finesse with the ten or put up the queen?

****

Considering the suit in isolation, the queen is the percentage play. Moreover, the defenders' discards, which I didn't specify, may suggest the winning play. But I would bank on an inference from West's defense. Suppose West had two trump entries plus a low trump, a doubleton heart and a weakish hand. To try for a heart ruff would have been a tempting defensive plan. He could win the first trump, lead his second heart, win the next trump and try to put his partner in for a heart ruff.

Since nothing of the sort happened, play West for three hearts.

```
♠ A K 6              ♠ 5
♥ J 6 4              ♥ 9 8 7
♦ 10 8 6 2           ♦ A J 9 4 3
♣ J 8 6              ♣ K Q 9 3
```

182

Dlr: South   ♠ Q 6
Vul: N-S   ♥ 7 4 3 2
                  ♦ A Q 3 2
                  ♣ Q 5 4

                  ♠ A 8 3
                  ♥ K J 6
                  ♦ K J 6 5
                  ♣ K J 2

WEST	NORTH	EAST	SOUTH
			1 NT
Pass	3 NT	All Pass	

West leads the ♠7, and you exhale when dummy's queen holds. If you can steal a heart trick, you can force out the ♣A for nine tricks in all. Suppose you lead a heart from dummy at trick two, declining to run the diamonds first. East plays the five.

King or jack?

****

I advise playing the jack.

Suppose East had the ♥A and West had the ♣A. A capable East would step up with his ace in order to return a spade, setting up the suit while West retained his entry (or letting West run the spades before declarer stole a ninth trick).

As against that, if you put up the ♥K, West might duck if he holds the ace but not the queen, keeping his entry. But I believe the case for playing the jack is stronger.

      ♠ K J 9 7 2   ♠ 10 5 4
      ♥ A 10 8   ♥ Q 9 5
      ♦ 8 7   ♦ 10 9 4
      ♣ 7 6 3   ♣ A 10 9 8

```
Dlr: South          ♠ K 5 3
Vul: Both           ♥ A Q 4 2
                    ♦ 10 9 2
                    ♣ 10 6 3


                    ♠ Q J 4
                    ♥ K 6 3
                    ♦ A K Q 8
                    ♣ Q 5 4
```

WEST	NORTH	EAST	SOUTH
			1 NT
Pass	2♣	Pass	2♦
Pass	3 NT	All Pass	

West leads the ♠6, and East takes the ace and shifts to the ♣J. That looks like an "honor-trapping" lead from K-J-9, so you play low from your hand (prepared to pay off if East has A-K-J-9). East continues with a low club, and West takes the ace and leads a second spade to your queen.

Next, you take your three hearts, and East discards a club. You cash the ♦AK, being careful to unblock dummy's nine and ten. Both defenders play low, and when you lead to the ♠K, East throws another club. At trick 11, dummy leads a diamond, and East follows low.

Which diamond do you play from your hand?

****

If you find this a problem, you had better review earlier chapters. You have a complete count: West started with five spades, four hearts and two clubs, hence two diamonds. Finesse with the ♦8.

```
      ♠ 10 8 7 6 2            ♠ A 9
      ♥ J 9 7 5              ♥ 10 8
      ♦ 5 3                  ♦ J 7 6 4
      ♣ A 7                  ♣ K J 9 8 2
```

Dlr: North
Vul: Both

```
              ♠ 9 4
              ♥ K 7 6 4
              ♦ J 9 6 5
              ♣ K 7 4


              ♠ A Q
              ♥ J 10 5 3 2
              ♦ A K Q 10
              ♣ 8 3
```

WEST	NORTH	EAST	SOUTH
	Pass	Pass	1♥
Pass	2♥	2♠	3♦
3♠	4♥	All Pass	

West leads the ♠8, and you win with the queen.

How do you play the trumps?

****

Give East the ♣A; barring a horrible trump break, your contract is safe if West has it. But East is marked with the ♠KJ10 and didn't open the bidding, so you can assume that West has the ♥A. Lead a low trump to dummy's king.

```
  ♠ 8 7 3 2              ♠ K J 10 6 5
  ♥ A 8                  ♥ Q 9
  ♦ 7 4                  ♦ 8 3 2
  ♣ Q J 6 5 2            ♣ A 10 9
```

An alternative would be to lead to the ♣K at trick two to find out who has the ♣A. But as the East-West cards lie, East could take the ♣A and continue with the ♣10 and a third club. When you ruffed and led a trump, West could (and should) rise with the ♥A to lead a fourth club, promoting East's ♥Q.

Dlr: South   ♠ K Q 10 4
Vul: N-S   ♥ A 4
                 ♦ A 9 3 2
                 ♣ 6 5 4

                 ♠ A 2
                 ♥ K 7 6
                 ♦ K Q 4
                 ♣ K J 7 3 2

WEST	NORTH	EAST	SOUTH
			1 NT
Pass	2♣	Pass	2♦
Pass	3 NT	All Pass	

West leads the ♥5. You win with dummy's ace and lead a club. When Esat plays the eight, you judge to put up the king. West takes the ace, alas, and leads the ♥2. He appears to have had a five-card suit. You duck East's jack and win the third heart, pitching a club from dummy.

Next you cash your three high spades. Both defenders follow low. When you continue with the ♦KQ, West plays the five and seven, East the six and ten. On a third diamond, West plays the eight.

Do you finesse with dummy's nine or put up the ace?

****

The concept of "restricted choice" suggests that you finesse. If East had J-10-6, he could have played either the ten or jack on the second diamond. Assuming he would play equal cards at random, his play of one honor lets you presume that he doesn't have the other.

Nevertheless, you should put up the ♦A here. Suppose East shows out. Then West will have started with three spades, five hearts and four diamonds, and his ♣A was singleton. So you can safely lead a second club toward your hand. East can take the ♣Q and cash the ♠J, but he will have to give you the 13th trick -- your ninth trick -- with the ♣J.

     ♠ 9 7 5   ♠ J 8 6 3
     ♥ Q 10 8 5 2   ♥ J 9 3
     ♦ 8 7 5   ♦ J 10 6
     ♣ A Q   ♣ 10 9 8

You can never lose your contract by playing the ♦A, but you could lose it by finessing with the nine.

CHAPTER 12

The inferential count

The techniques of counting and inference are often combined. Indeed, a player who must make a crucial decision before he can assemble a picture of the deal often relies on inference.

When declarer has a guess, he prefers to postpone it. He digs for information by playing the other suits. But if declarer has a guess in trumps, to delay may be risky or pointless.

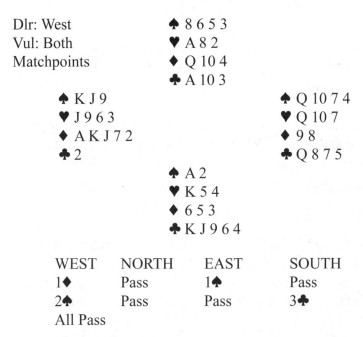

	Dlr: West	♠ 8 6 5 3	
	Vul: Both	♥ A 8 2	
	Matchpoints	♦ Q 10 4	
		♣ A 10 3	

♠ K J 9	♠ Q 10 7 4
♥ J 9 6 3	♥ Q 10 7
♦ A K J 7 2	♦ 9 8
♣ 2	♣ Q 8 7 5

	♠ A 2
	♥ K 5 4
	♦ 6 5 3
	♣ K J 9 6 4

WEST	NORTH	EAST	SOUTH
1♦	Pass	1♠	Pass
2♠	Pass	Pass	3♣
All Pass			

When East-West stop at the two level, North is marked with some values. At the vulnerability, South's balancing 3♣ is still extreme; North need not have club support. But at matchpoints, players often try to beat par in the auction by indulging in risky actions.

West leads two top diamonds and gives East a diamond ruff. South wins a spade shift and must guess right in trumps to get out for down one. Down two, -200, will be a matchpoint disaster.

South knows West had five diamonds, East two. East needed four spades for his 1♠ response, but West needed three-card support to raise. Hearts? If East had four, he would have responded 1♥; if he had two, West would have had five and would have opened 1♥.

Since East's pattern must have been 4-3-2-4, declarer can take the ♣A and let the ten ride.

Dlr: East   ♠ J 3
Vul: N-S   ♥ K Q 4
                     ♦ K 8 4 2
                     ♣ J 9 5 3

                     ♠ K Q 9 8 4 2
                     ♥ A 8 2
                     ♦ 7 5 3
                     ♣ A

WEST	NORTH	EAST	SOUTH
		1♣	1♠
2♣	2 NT	Pass	4♠
All Pass			

West leads the ♦Q, and when dummy plays low, the ace appears from East. He shifts to the ♣2, and you take the ace and lead a trump to dummy's jack. East wins and leads another club, which you ruff.

How do you continue?

****

The East-West clubs must be divided 4-4. West would not have raised with fewer than four, but if East had only three plus the singleton ♦A, he would have had five cards in a major. In fact, East's pattern must be 4-4-1-4. Lead a heart to dummy and return a trump to your nine.

    ♠ 5   ♠ A 10 7 6
    ♥ 10 6 5   ♥ J 9 7 3
    ♦ Q J 10 9 6   ♦ A
    ♣ Q 8 7 4   ♣ K 10 6 2

```
Dlr: West          ♠ K 6 5 3
Vul: None          ♥ 5 4 3
Matchpoints        ♦ K 10 7 2
                   ♣ K 3


                   ♠ A 4 2
                   ♥ K J 9
                   ♦ A J 9 3
                   ♣ J 6 4
```

WEST	NORTH	EAST	SOUTH
Pass	Pass	Pass	1♦
Pass	1♠	Pass	1 NT
All Pass			

At IMPs North might have corrected to 2♦, probably a safer contract. At matchpoints he couldn't afford to accept +110 at diamonds if notrump would produce eight tricks for +120.

West leads the ♥6, and East takes the ace and returns the ten. You try the jack without much hope, and West wins with the queen. You await a third heart, but West ponders and shifts to the ♠J.

How do you play the diamonds?

****

West's defense is odd, but he had a reason -- that seemed logical to him -- for shifting. West might have held either four or five hearts, but if he had a certain side entry, presumably he would have continued hearts.

So you can place East with the ♣A, the ♥A, and the ♠Q (since West led the ♠J). Not many Easts would pass a 12-point hand with two aces in third position at matchpoints, so the ♦Q should lie with West.

```
    ♠ J 10                    ♠ Q 9 8 7
    ♥ Q 8 7 6 2               ♥ A 10
    ♦ Q 5 4                   ♦ 8 6
    ♣ Q 10 8                  ♣ A 9 7 5 2
```

After you take four diamond tricks, you can make an overtrick by throwing East in with a spade to give dummy the ♣K.

```
Dlr: South          ♠ 8 7 3
Vul: N-S            ♥ K 10 4 2
                    ♦ K 6 5
                    ♣ 7 5 2


                    ♠ K 10 5
                    ♥ A Q 3
                    ♦ J 8 3
                    ♣ A K Q 10
```

WEST	NORTH	EAST	SOUTH
			1♣
Pass	1♥	Pass	2 NT
Pass	3 NT	All Pass	

West leads the ♠2: three, jack, king. When you cash the ♣AK, West discards a diamond.

How do you play the hearts?

****

West had one club, and his lead of the ♠2 indicated a four-card suit. If West had a five-card diamond suit, he would -- most probably -- have led a diamond. Play West for four hearts. Cash the ♥AQ and lead a third heart. If no jack appears, finesse with dummy's ten.

```
♠ A Q 6 2              ♠ J 9 4
♥ J 7 6 5              ♥ 9 8
♦ Q 9 7 2              ♦ A 10 4
♣ 3                    ♣ J 9 8 6 4
```

Four heart tricks, a spade and four clubs will land the contract.

Dlr: West   ♠ 5 4
Vul: Both   ♥ A J 7 4
                   ◆ J 6 5 3
                   ♣ 8 5 3

                   ♠ K J 2
                   ♥ Q 10 8 5 3 2
                   ◆ A K 10
                   ♣ Q

WEST	NORTH	EAST	SOUTH
Pass	Pass	Pass	1♥
Dbl	2♥	2♠	3♥
All Pass			

West leads the ♣K and continues with the ♣A, which you ruff. You will go down at 3♥ only if you misguess everything in sight.

Plan the play. For starters, do you finesse in trumps?

****

Lead a trump to the ace. If both defenders play low, ruff dummy's last club and exit with a trump. If West has the king, East will probably have both the ♠A and ◆Q since West might have opened the bidding with the ♥K, the ♣AK and another king or queen. So you will make an overtrick, losing a trump, a club and a spade. (If you happened to reach 4♥, you might play the same way.)

If East wins the second trump and puts you to a guess by leading a low spade, play the king. If West wins, you will lose another spade, but the diamond finesse will work since West would have opened with the ♣AK, ♠A and ◆Q.

       ♠ Q 9 6 3   ♠ A 10 8 7
       ♥ 9 6   ♥ K
       ◆ Q 9 4   ◆ 8 7 2
       ♣ A K 10 2   ♣ J 9 7 6 4

East-West could have given you a tough decision by competing to 3♠.

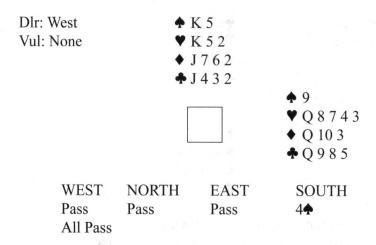

Dlr: West
Vul: None

♠ K 5
♥ K 5 2
♦ J 7 6 2
♣ J 4 3 2

♠ 9
♥ Q 8 7 4 3
♦ Q 10 3
♣ Q 9 8 5

WEST	NORTH	EAST	SOUTH
Pass	Pass	Pass	4♠
All Pass			

West leads the ♥10, and when dummy plays low, you follow with the three. Declarer takes the jack and continues with the ♠A, ♥A and ♠K. You discard a heart. South discards a diamond on the ♥K and leads a club to his king and West's ace.

West next leads the ♣10. Low from dummy. How do you defend?

****

South had two hearts. If he had eight spades, he is making an overtrick, so assume he had a seven-card suit. He can't have had a low singleton diamond since West would have led a high diamond from A-K-x-x. Nor can South have held three diamonds and one club; then he would have pitched his singleton ♣K on the third heart and tried to develop a diamond trick.

So you can place declarer with 7-2-2-2 distribution. Overtake partner's ♣10 with the queen and lead a fourth heart.

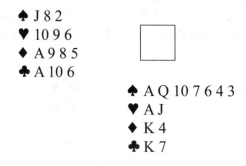

♠ J 8 2
♥ 10 9 6
♦ A 9 8 5
♣ A 10 6

♠ A Q 10 7 6 4 3
♥ A J
♦ K 4
♣ K 7

South can postpone his demise by discarding the ♦K, but West will discard his last club. Then you will lead a club, promoting West's ♠J for the setting trick.

```
Dlr: South          ♠ 6 3
Vul: N-S            ♥ Q 10 7 4
                    ♦ K J 9 4
                    ♣ A 9 5
                                        ♠ Q 10 5 2
                                        ♥ 3 2
                                        ♦ A 8 5 3
                                        ♣ J 8 2
```

WEST	NORTH	EAST	SOUTH
			1NT
Pass	2♣	Pass	2♠
Pass	3 NT	Pass	4♥
All Pass			

West leads the ♦10, and declarer calls for dummy's king.

How do you defend?

****

This is a breather of a problem. West's ♦10 can't be a singleton. That would give South four diamonds as well as four cards in each major; he wouldn't have opened 1NT with 4-4-4-1 pattern. Signal with the ♦8, playing West for a doubleton diamond and a fast re-entry in trumps.

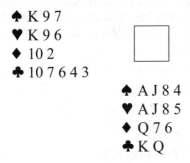

```
♠ K 9 7
♥ K 9 6
♦ 10 2
♣ 10 7 6 4 3
                    ♠ A J 8 4
                    ♥ A J 8 5
                    ♦ Q 7 6
                    ♣ K Q
```

When I pose this problem in a lecture, I sometimes hear a question like, "What if South opened 1NT with, say, the singleton ♣K? Then my partner will kill me if I don't give him a diamond ruff."

That is a case of what I call the "What If" syndrome. A player is so worried about a bizarre lie of the cards that he bases his play on that lie instead of one that is overwhelmingly more likely. Sure, I have seen and read accounts of deals where a player opened 1NT with an off-shape hand, but defenders can't go assuming that declarer has blithely violated his system.

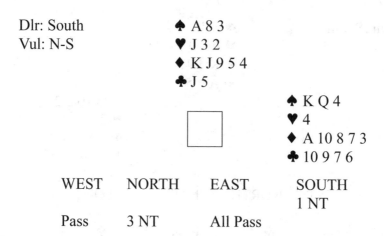

Dlr: South ♠ A 8 3
Vul: N-S ♥ J 3 2
♦ K J 9 5 4
♣ J 5

♠ K Q 4
♥ 4
♦ A 10 8 7 3
♣ 10 9 7 6

WEST	NORTH	EAST	SOUTH
			1 NT
Pass	3 NT	All Pass	

West leads the ♠2, ducked to your queen. You return the ♠K, also ducked, and a third spade. All follow, and dummy's ace wins. At trick four, dummy leads the ♦4.

How do you defend?

****

West led from a four-card spade suit, so you can infer that he has a singleton diamond, otherwise he would have had a five-card suit from which to lead. West's pattern should be 4-4-1-4, leaving South with 3-5-2-3.

To rise with the ♦A will not cost a trick directly since declarer's winners will be tangled. When you do that, South and West play low as you expect. What do you lead next?

****

Lead the ♣10. The only danger is that South has all the heart honors. He can never take nine tricks if West has a heart entry. But a heart return would be fatal against the actual lie of the West and South cards:

♠ J 10 6 2
♥ 10 9 8 7
♦ 2
♣ A 4 3 2

♠ 9 7 5
♥ A K Q 6 5
♦ Q 6
♣ K Q 8

Moreover, if you don't grab the first diamond, South can get home by forcing out West's ♣A next. You will eat your ♦A.

Not every player would have opened 1NT. Many players absolutely refuse to suppress a strong five-card major. Others prefer to describe a hand's general strength and pattern in one bid. After a 1♥ opening and a 1♠ response, South would lack a descriptive second bid. Either style may gain on a given deal.

```
Dlr: East          ♠ 6 4
Vul: None          ♥ K J 10 3
                   ♦ Q 10 5
                   ♣ A J 9 4


                   ♠ A Q 7 2
                   ♥ Q 5
                   ♦ 7 6 3
                   ♣ K 10 6 3
```

WEST	NORTH	EAST	SOUTH
		1♦	Pass
1♠	Pass	2♠	Pass
Pass	Dbl	Pass	3♣
All Pass			

When East-West come to rest at 2♠, North balances fearlessly. Against your 3♣, West leads the ♦K, then the ♦J. You cover with dummy's queen, and East takes the ace and returns a third diamond. West ruffs and shifts to the ♠3: four, king, ace.

You still have the ♥A to lose, but you will make your contract if you pick up the trumps. Whom do you play for the queen?

****

East needed three-card spade support for his raise, so West had only a four-card suit. East had five diamonds, West had two. East had four hearts: West would have responded up-the-line with 1♥ if he had four, and East would have opened 1♥ with five.

Put it all together. East's pattern was 3-4-5-1. Cash the ♣K and lead to dummy's jack.

```
♠ J 9 8 3              ♠ K 10 5
♥ 9 8 6                ♥ A 7 4 2
♦ K J                  ♦ A 9 8 4 2
♣ Q 8 7 2              ♣ 5
```

At matchpoints you might have taken a chance and passed North's double for penalty. In fact, perfect defense would collect +300 against 2♠ doubled, but North could have had a weaker hand. At IMPs, to pass was too close; it risked -470.

Dlr: East   ♠ Q 8 4
Vul: None   ♥ 6 5 3
        ♦ 6 5 4
        ♣ A K 10 5

        ♠ K J 9 6
        ♥ 9 8 7
        ♦ A K 9
        ♣ Q 4 3

WEST	NORTH	EAST	SOUTH
		1♦	Pass
2♦	Pass	Pass	2♠
All Pass			

Some players would have doubled 1♦ with the South cards. Failing that, to balance with a double over 2♦ would be normal; to sell out to 2♦ when East-West have found a fit and North is marked with some values would be defeatist. But suppose your partner's dummy play is suspect, and you would rather take your chances at 2♠ than see him at the wheel at 2♥ or 3♣.

West leads the ♦2, East plays the jack and you take the king. You lead a trump to dummy's queen, and East takes the ace and returns the ♦8 to your ace. How do you continue?

****

East had three diamonds. The play to the first trick marks West with the ♦10, and he wouldn't have raised with 10-7-2. East had four hearts; West would have responded 1♥ with four.

It's possible that East opened 1♦ with 3-4-3-3 pattern -- some players open in the stronger minor with that -- but with a weak holding in both minors, most players open 1♣. "Prepared" three-card 1♣ openings are awkward enough; nobody likes three-card 1♦ openings. Moreover, East had a skinny opening bid. Having two four-card majors would have made his hand more attractive.

Play East for 4-4-3-2 distribution. Cash your ♠K, lead a club to dummy and return a trump to your nine. After you draw the last trump, take the ♣Q and lead a third club to the ten.

♠ 7 2	♠ A 10 5 3
♥ K 10 2	♥ A Q J 4
♦ Q 10 7 2	♦ J 8 3
♣ J 9 8 2	♣ 7 6

If you win nine tricks for +140, your partner will forgive you for hogging the play.

East would have done better to duck the first trump.

Dlr: East   ♠ J 7 5 4
Vul: Both   ♥ Q 10 6 3
Matchpoints   ♦ A 10 4
              ♣ J 7

              ♠
              ♥ J 7 2
              ♦ J 7 5
              ♣ A K 8 6 5 4 3

WEST	NORTH	EAST	SOUTH
		1♦	3♣
Pass	Pass	Dbl	All Pass

West leads the ♦2. When dummy plays low, East wins with the king and tries to cash the ♠K. You ruff.

How do you continue?

****

If West has all four missing trumps, you need to lead a trump toward dummy's J-7 to hold your trump losers to one. But West's opening lead and East's play of the ♦K indicate that West held at least three diamonds and East no more than four. If East had a five-card major, he would have opened in it, so East must have at least one club.

Cash the ♣AK, expecting to lose a diamond, a trump and two hearts.

♠ Q 10 8 6 2   ♠ A K 9 3
♥ A 4   ♥ K 9 8 5
♦ Q 6 2   ♦ K 9 8 3
♣ Q 10 9   ♣ 2

If you lead a low trump, West will take his queen, shift to the ♥A and a low heart, and get a heart ruff to defeat you.

(Winning play attributed to Marshall Miles, who observed that West's unorthodox penalty pass would result in +200 unless declarer was alert.)

```
Dlr: East          ♠ 8 7 4 2
Vul: None          ♥ A 10 6 5
                   ♦ K Q 7
                   ♣ K 3


                   ♠ A Q 10 6 3
                   ♥ 7
                   ♦ 9 5
                   ♣ Q J 10 8 7
```

WEST	NORTH	EAST	SOUTH
		1♣	1♠
2♦	3♣	Pass	3♠
Pass	4♠	All Pass	

After East opened 1♣, North's ♣K was a doubtful value, so his decision to drive to game was questionable.

West leads the ♣9, and East takes the ace and shifts to a diamond. West wins and returns the ♦J, and East ruffs dummy's queen with the ♠5. When a club comes back, you steel yourself for another ruff, but West follows with the five, and dummy's king wins.

How do you play the trumps?

****

East had one diamond and clearly four clubs. He would have opened in a five-card major, hence his pattern was 4-4-1-4. Lead a trump to your ten.

```
♠                      ♠ K J 9 5
♥ Q 8 4 3              ♥ K J 9 2
♦ A J 10 8 6 4 3       ♦ 2
♣ 9 5                  ♣ A 6 4 2
```

When the ten wins, you can return to dummy with the ♥A to pick up the trumps with a second finesse and claim your game.

Dlr: East
Vul: None

♠ A J 7 4
♥ 10 6 4
♦ J 5 3
♣ K 7 3

♠ Q 10 8 6 3 2
♥ K 5
♦ 9 6 4
♣ A 5

WEST	NORTH	EAST	SOUTH
		Pass	Pass
1♦	Pass	2♣	2♠
3♣	3♠	All Pass	

West leads the ♦K and ♦A, dropping East's queen. East ruffs the third diamond and shifts to the ♥A and ♥2. Your king wins.

How do you play the trumps?

****

West had five diamonds, East had two. The missing hearts must be split 4-4, else someone would have bid the suit. If the clubs are also 4-4, East had three trumps and you must lose another trump to his king. But East surely has five clubs (and West raised with three-card support) since East would respond 1♥ with K95,A982,Q8,J1086.

Lead a trump to the ace.

♠ 5	♠ K 9
♥ Q 9 7 3	♥ A J 8 2
♦ A K 10 7 2	♦ Q 8
♣ Q 9 2	♣ J 10 8 6 4

East-West compressed their five winners into four, but many defenders would have done the same.

Dlr: South   ♠ 9 5 3
Vul: N-S   ♥ A 9 6
Matchpoints   ♦ K J 9 3
                   ♣ K 4 2

                   ♠ A Q 10
                   ♥ 7 4
                   ♦ A 6 5 2
                   ♣ A Q 5 3

WEST   NORTH   EAST   SOUTH
                           1 NT
Pass   3 NT   All Pass

West leads the ♠2, and East puts up the king, losing to your ace. The contract is "normal" -- every North-South will be at 3NT -- so you need to make the maximum. Suppose you take your three high clubs, and West discards the ♥5.

How do you play the diamonds?

****

West had two clubs. He probably had ♠Jxxx and those spots were poor. If he had four hearts, almost surely they would have been stronger than his spades. Quite probably, West's pattern was 4-3-4-2.

        ♠ J 7 6 2   ♠ K 8 4
        ♥ J 8 5   ♥ K Q 10 3 2
        ♦ Q 10 7 4   ♦ 8
        ♣ 7 6   ♣ J 10 9 8

To take the ♦A and follow with a diamond to dummy's nine requires the courage of your convictions but will be worth a top here. Note that your play will break even if East happens to have Q-x since you would have lost one diamond trick anyway.

Dlr: West ♠ K 6 5
Vul: None ♥ 10 8 5 4
           ♦ 10 9 5 2
           ♣ Q 4

           ♠ Q 10 4 3
           ♥ A 2
           ♦ K 3
           ♣ A K 10 6 3

WEST	NORTH	EAST	SOUTH
1♦	Pass	1♥	2♣
2♥	Pass	Pass	Dbl
Pass	3♣	All Pass	

As South, you overcalled at your first turn instead of doubling because you wanted to get your five-card suit mentioned.

Against 3♣, West leads the ♥Q. You take the ace and correctly attack your side suit. A spade to dummy's king wins, and a spade to your ten loses to West's ace. Good. West cashes the ♥J and exits with a third spade to East's jack and your queen.

You still have two diamonds to lose -- West will hold the ♦A -- but you can make 3♣ if you pick up the trumps. How do you proceed?

****

West had one of two possible hands: A9x,QJx,AQxxx,xx or A9x,QJx,AQxx,xxx. The first hand looks more likely for his raise to 2♥. With the second hand -- minimum high-card values and no shape -- he might have been more inclined to pass.

Follow the odds. Take the ♣Q and lead a club to your ten.

♠ A 9 7   ♠ J 8 2
♥ Q J 9   ♥ K 7 6 3
♦ A Q 8 7 6   ♦ J 4
♣ 8 5   ♣ J 9 7 2

Some Wests would have made a conventional "support double" over your 2♣, showing three-card heart support. A raise to 2♥ would have promised four-card support. I am not a fan of that convention -- the rest of the auction is often murky, and the ability to penalize the overcaller is compromised -- but many players see an advantage in defining the quality of their support.

```
Dlr: West              ♠ Q 10
Vul: E-W               ♥ 7 6 5 2
                       ♦ 7 6 3
                       ♣ 8 7 6 2


                       ♠ A K 9 6 4 3
                       ♥ A Q 3
                       ♦ Q 2
                       ♣ Q J
```

WEST	NORTH	EAST	SOUTH
1 NT	Pass	2♦	Dbl
Pass	2♥	Pass	2♠
All Pass			

East's 2♦ run-out was natural. Against your 2♠, West leads the ♣K and then the ♣A. East plays the three and five, and West leads a third club to East's ten. You ruff.

How do you proceed?

****

It appears that West had four clubs, and he probably had three diamonds. If East had a six-card suit, he might have competed to 3♦, and West might have led or shifted to diamonds.

To make 2♠, you need a second heart trick. East should hold a diamond honor since West might have led or shifted to diamonds otherwise. So West will have the ♥K, and you must hope he has K-x.

Play West for 4-2-3-4 pattern. At the fourth trick, lead a trump to dummy's ten. Cash the queen, come to your ♥A and draw trumps. Then lead a low heart and hope your picture of the deal is on target.

```
♠ J 8 7 2              ♠ 5
♥ K 9                  ♥ J 10 8 4
♦ A J 5                ♦ K 10 9 8 4
♣ A K 9 4              ♣ 10 5 3
```

The problem illustrates what more accurately might be called a "hypothetical" count. You must presume that the cards lie in a specific way.

East-West seem to have gone too quietly. They could have made 3NT by West or 5♦.

LAST CHANCE

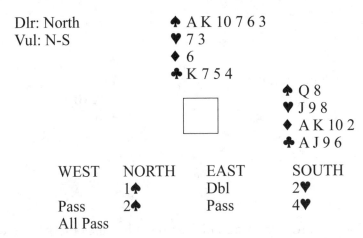

Dlr: North
Vul: N-S

♠ A K 10 7 6 3
♥ 7 3
♦ 6
♣ K 7 5 4

♠ Q 8
♥ J 9 8
♦ A K 10 2
♣ A J 9 6

WEST	NORTH	EAST	SOUTH
	1♠	Dbl	2♥
Pass	2♠	Pass	4♥
All Pass			

West leads the ♦4, you win with the king and South follows with the five. When you shift to a trump, South takes the ace and leads a spade: four, ten, queen.

How do you defend?

****

South has at least three diamonds and has two spades to attack the spades in such a manner. If he had a seven-card trump suit, he would have ruffed a diamond in dummy for 10 tricks, so give him a six-card suit. He didn't ruff a diamond in dummy because it wouldn't help him come to 10 tricks; he must be relying instead on the spades.

Return a spade, cutting his link with dummy.

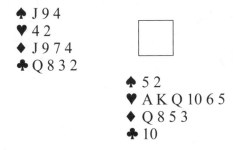

♠ J 9 4
♥ 4 2
♦ J 9 7 4
♣ Q 8 3 2

♠ 5 2
♥ A K Q 10 6 5
♦ Q 8 5 3
♣ 10

The spade return beats 4♥. In fact, East could also beat it by cashing the ♣A, then returning a spade, or even by leading the ♦A.

The play would be interesting if South ruffed a diamond at the third trick and led a club from dummy. To prevail, West would have to win and lead a spade. On any other defense, East would fall victim to a three-suit squeeze.

After a diamond opening lead and a trump shift, South could always make his game. He ruffs a diamond, takes the ♠AK, ruffs a spade and runs his trumps. With three tricks to go and South needing one more trick, the position is

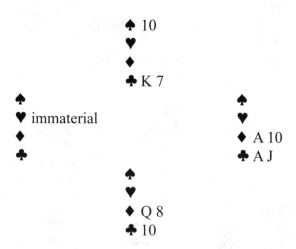

```
            ♠ 10
            ♥
            ♦
            ♣ K 7
♠                          ♠
♥ immaterial               ♥
♦                          ♦ A 10
♣                          ♣ A J
            ♠
            ♥
            ♦ Q 8
            ♣ 10
```

East, still to discard, can turn in his sword. If he bares the ♦A, he will be thrown in with it to concede a trick to dummy's ♣K. If East bares his ♣A, he will be thrown in with it to give South his ♦Q at the 13th trick.

What a game of beautiful complexity we play.

About the Author

Frank Stewart (b. 1946) is one of the world's most prolific bridge journalists, known as an advocate of a sound and disciplined approach to bidding. He won many tournament events before devoting himself to writing. Stewart served as co-editor of the ACBL's Bridge Bulletin 1984-1989 and continues to contribute through an instructional column he began in 1981. He edited the ACBL's World Championship books 1983-1987 and was a principal contributor 1986-1989. He was a principal contributor to the Fifth Edition of "The Official Encyclopedia of Bridge."

In 1986 Stewart began a collaboration with Alfred Sheinwold to produce the syndicated newspaper column "Sheinwold on Bridge." After Sheinwold's death in 1997, the column continued under Stewart's byline as "Sheinwold's Bridge" and in 2000 became "Daily Bridge Club." It appears in newspapers worldwide and on major internet sites.

Stewart has published hundreds of magazine and on-line articles including technical pieces, tournament reports, fiction and humor. He has written 20 other books, among them "Becoming an Expert," "Frank Stewart's Bridge Club" and "Frank Stewart's World of Bridge." He has been an analyst for ACBL-wide Charity and International Fund events since 1980.

Stewart is a graduate of the University of Alabama where he studied voice and musicology. He is a low-handicap golfer and a past chairman of the Fayette Christian Center of Concern, a food bank. He and his wife, Charlotte, a pediatric speech pathologist, live in Fayette AL. They have an 11-year-old daughter.